Excel Mastery 2025: From Beginner to Pro in 30 Days

A Step-by-Step Guide to unlock Excel full Functions, Formulas, Shortcuts and Advanced Techniques

Thomas T. Haws

Table of Contents

Introduction

Welcome to *Excel Mastery,* a comprehensive guide designed to help you harness the full power of Microsoft Excel. Whether you're stepping into the world of spreadsheets for the first time or looking to sharpen your existing skills, this book serves as a structured roadmap that will transform you into a proficient Excel user.

Microsoft Excel is far more than just a spreadsheet application; it is a multifaceted tool that enables users to efficiently manage data, perform complex calculations, analyze trends, create dynamic visualizations, and even automate repetitive tasks.

Over the decades, Excel has solidified its place as an indispensable resource across multiple industries, from finance and business management to data science, engineering, and creative disciplines. Its ability to streamline workflows, enhance productivity, and support informed decision-making makes it a must-have skill in today's data-driven world.

This book has been meticulously crafted to provide a hands-on, practical learning experience. Each chapter is designed to introduce key Excel concepts progressively, ensuring that beginners build a strong foundation while allowing experienced users to refine their techniques. By the time you reach the final chapter, you will not only be comfortable navigating Excel but also confident in utilizing its advanced features to optimize your workflow and improve efficiency.

How This Book is Structured

To facilitate a smooth and engaging learning process, this book follows a carefully organized, step-by-step approach. Each chapter builds upon the previous one, ensuring a logical progression from basic operations to more sophisticated techniques. The content is structured into a four-week learning plan, covering everything from fundamental Excel functions to automation, data analysis, and AI-powered enhancements.

Key Features of This Book:

- Structured Learning Path: Concepts are presented in a logical sequence, helping you build expertise step by step.

- Hands-on Exercises: Each chapter includes practical exercises with sample datasets to reinforce learning through real-world application.

- Latest Excel Features: Stay up to date with the newest capabilities, including Excel 365, Power Query, Power Pivot, and AI-driven Copilot.

- Practical Applications: Discover how Excel is used in real-world scenarios such as financial modeling, project management, and data visualization.

- Time-Saving Shortcuts: Learn essential productivity hacks and keyboard shortcuts to work faster and smarter.

How to Maximize Your Learning Experience:

- Follow the Progression: Start with the basics and advance through the chapters systematically to build a solid foundation.
- Practice as You Go: Download the sample datasets provided and replicate the exercises on your own Excel software.
- Use as a Reference Guide: Beyond learning, this book can serve as a go-to resource whenever you need to revisit key Excel functions.
- Apply Knowledge to Real-World Scenarios: Reinforce your learning by integrating Excel into your daily personal and professional tasks.
- By the time you complete this book, you'll have developed a strong command of Excel, allowing you to tackle everyday tasks more

efficiently and take on complex projects with confidence.

A Brief History of Microsoft Excel

Since its inception, Microsoft Excel has undergone significant transformations, evolving into the robust, feature-rich tool that professionals rely on today. Originally introduced in 1985 for Macintosh, Excel was later released for Windows in 1987, quickly becoming a dominant force in the spreadsheet software market. Over the decades, Microsoft has continually enhanced Excel, integrating cutting-edge technologies to meet the ever-growing demands of users worldwide.

Key Milestones in Excel's Evolution:

- **1985:** Excel 1.0 was launched exclusively for Macintosh users, introducing basic spreadsheet functions.
- **1987:** The first Windows-compatible version of Excel was released, making it accessible to a broader audience.

- **1993:** Excel 5.0 introduced VBA (Visual Basic for Applications), revolutionizing automation through macros.

- **2003:** The introduction of XML support improved data compatibility and sharing capabilities.

- **2007:** Microsoft redesigned Excel's interface, introducing the Ribbon toolbar and transitioning from .xls to .xlsx file formats.

- **2010:** PowerPivot was introduced, providing enhanced data modeling and large-scale data processing capabilities.

- **2013-2016:** Significant enhancements in Power Query and Power BI integration allowed for seamless data transformation and visualization.

- **2020-Present:** AI-powered features such as Excel Copilot, Python integration, and dynamic arrays expanded Excel's capabilities, making data analysis more intuitive and automated.

Why Excel is More Relevant Than Ever

In an era where data plays a critical role in decision-making, Microsoft Excel remains one of the most widely used and versatile tools in business, finance, research, and education. Its adaptability and continuous innovation ensure that it remains an essential skill for professionals across industries.

With the advent of cloud computing, Excel has evolved beyond a traditional desktop application. It now seamlessly integrates with cloud-based solutions such as OneDrive, SharePoint, and Power BI, allowing users to collaborate in real time and access their work from anywhere. Additionally, Microsoft's AI-driven Copilot feature is transforming how users interact with data by automating repetitive tasks, generating insights, and simplifying complex calculations using natural language processing.

Looking to the Future

As Excel continues to evolve, staying updated with its latest features will give you a competitive edge in the workplace. By mastering Excel, you are equipping yourself with a high-value skill set that enhances efficiency, supports data-driven decision-making, and opens doors to career opportunities in various fields.

This book is your gateway to becoming proficient in Excel, ensuring you stay ahead of the curve with up-to-date knowledge and practical applications. So, let's begin your journey toward Excel mastery and take your spreadsheet skills to the next level!

Week 1: Foundations of Excel

Chapter 1: Getting Started with Excel

Introduction

Microsoft Excel is an essential tool used by millions worldwide for organizing, analyzing, and presenting data. Whether you're a student managing assignments, a business professional handling financial reports, or someone tracking personal expenses, Excel provides an intuitive yet highly functional environment to help streamline tasks. Its widespread application in industries such as finance, education, business management, and data analytics highlights its versatility and importance in the modern digital world.

This chapter serves as your foundational guide to Excel, covering the fundamental elements such as navigating the interface, understanding workbooks and worksheets, and customizing the Quick Access

Toolbar. By the end of this chapter, you will have developed a strong understanding of Excel's layout and essential functions, allowing you to work efficiently and with confidence.

Navigating the Excel Interface

When you launch Excel, you are greeted with a structured and user-friendly interface. Mastering the various components of this interface is crucial for maximizing efficiency and making full use of Excel's extensive features.

1. The Ribbon

The Ribbon is the central hub for Excel's tools and commands. It is divided into multiple tabs, each containing groups of related functions:

- **File Tab**: Provides options for creating, opening, saving, printing, and sharing Excel files.
- **Home Tab**: Contains essential commands for formatting text, applying styles, adjusting

fonts, aligning data, and performing basic editing tasks.

- **Insert Tab**: Allows users to add tables, charts, pivot tables, images, and other elements to their spreadsheets.
- **Page Layout Tab**: Manages print settings, themes, margins, page orientation, and sheet scaling.
- **Formulas Tab**: Grants access to a wide array of built-in Excel functions and formula-related tools.
- **Data Tab**: Includes tools for importing, sorting, filtering, and analyzing data from various sources.
- **Review Tab**: Features spell check, comments, and track changes functionalities for collaborative work.
- **View Tab**: Controls display options such as zoom, gridlines, freeze panes, and window arrangement.

2. The Formula Bar

The Formula Bar is positioned above the worksheet grid and displays the content of the active cell. This tool is crucial for entering or modifying formulas, numbers, and text.

3. The Worksheet Grid

The worksheet grid is composed of rows (numbered) and columns (lettered). Each intersection forms a **cell**, which is the primary unit for data entry. Key elements of the grid include:

- **Active Cell**: The currently selected cell, highlighted with a bold outline.
- **Name Box**: Displays the reference of the active cell (e.g., A1, B3, C5).
- **Sheet Tabs**: Located at the bottom, allowing users to switch between different worksheets within a workbook.

4. The Status Bar

The Status Bar is located at the bottom of the Excel window and provides real-time information about selected data, such as sum, average, and count. It also contains options for zooming and changing the spreadsheet view.

5. The Quick Access Toolbar

Positioned in the top-left corner, the Quick Access Toolbar (QAT) provides shortcuts for frequently used commands like Save, Undo, and Redo. Users can customize this toolbar to include additional commands for increased productivity.

Understanding Workbooks and Worksheets

What is a Workbook?

A workbook is an Excel file that contains one or more worksheets. Think of a workbook as a digital binder that holds multiple sheets of data within a single file.

What is a Worksheet?

A worksheet is an individual spreadsheet within a workbook, composed of rows and columns used to organize and manipulate data.

Key Components of a Worksheet

- **Columns**: Labeled alphabetically (A, B, C... Z, AA, AB, etc.).
- **Rows**: Numbered sequentially (1, 2, 3, etc.).
- **Cells**: The intersection of a row and column (e.g., B2, C5).
- **Cell Address**: A unique identifier for each cell (e.g., A1, F10).

Range: A selection of multiple cells (e.g., A1:B5 represents a rectangular selection).

Working with Workbooks

- **Creating a New Workbook**: Click File > New > Blank Workbook.
- **Opening an Existing Workbook**: Click File > Open and browse for the file.
- **Saving a Workbook**:
  - Save as .xlsx for modern Excel files.
  - Save as .xls for compatibility with older versions.
  - Save as .csv for text-based data storage.

Managing Worksheets

- **Renaming a Worksheet**: Double-click the sheet tab and enter a new name.
- **Adding a New Worksheet**: Click the + icon next to the sheet tabs.
- **Deleting a Worksheet**: Right-click the sheet tab and select Delete.
- **Moving or Copying a Worksheet**: Right-click the sheet tab, choose Move or Copy, and select the destination.
- **Color Coding Tabs**: Right-click a sheet tab, select Tab Color, and choose a color for better organization.

Customizing the Quick Access Toolbar

The Quick Access Toolbar (QAT) is a time-saving feature that helps users streamline their workflow by providing quick access to commonly used commands.

Why Customize the Quick Access Toolbar?

By default, the QAT contains only a few essential commands, such as Save, Undo, and Redo. However, customizing it allows users to add frequently used tools, minimizing the need to navigate through the Ribbon.

Adding Commands to the Quick Access Toolbar

1. Click the small drop-down arrow at the right end of the Quick Access Toolbar.
2. Select **More Commands**.
3. In the Excel Options window, choose a command from the left panel.
4. Click **Add >>** to move it to the right panel.
5. Click **OK** to save changes.

Recommended Commands to Add

- **New File**: Quickly create a new workbook.
- **Open File**: Access existing workbooks instantly.
- **Print Preview**: Saves time when formatting documents for printing.
- **Sort & Filter**: Essential for data organization.

- **Format Painter**: Copies formatting from one cell to another.
- **AutoSum**: Instantly calculates the sum of selected cells.

Removing Commands from the Quick Access Toolbar

1. Click the drop-down arrow on the QAT.
2. Select **More Commands**.
3. Highlight the command in the right panel.
4. Click **Remove**.
5. Click **OK** to save changes.

Changing the Position of the Quick Access Toolbar

By default, the QAT appears above the Ribbon, but you can move it below the Ribbon for easier access:

1. Click the drop-down arrow.
2. Select **Show Below the Ribbon**.
3. To revert, click the drop-down arrow again and choose **Show Above the Ribbon**.

Conclusion

In this chapter, you have learned the fundamentals of Excel, including navigating the interface, managing workbooks and worksheets, and customizing the Quick Access Toolbar. These essential skills will serve as the foundation for exploring more advanced Excel functionalities in subsequent chapters.

Now that you're comfortable with the basics, the next chapter will focus on data entry and formatting, equipping you with the skills to input and structure data efficiently.

Chapter 2: Entering and Formatting Data

Microsoft Excel is a powerful tool designed to store, organize, and manipulate data efficiently. However, to take full advantage of its capabilities, it's essential to understand the best practices for entering and formatting data properly.

A well-structured spreadsheet not only enhances readability but also simplifies data analysis and reporting.

In this chapter, you'll learn how to input data efficiently, leverage automation tools like Autofill and Flash Fill, and apply formatting techniques to improve your spreadsheet's presentation. By the end, you'll have the skills to enter, structure, and format your data with confidence, setting the foundation for more advanced Excel tasks in later chapters.

Data Entry Techniques

Accurate and efficient data entry is fundamental to creating functional spreadsheets. Excel provides multiple ways to input and manage data, helping users save time while maintaining precision.

1. Manual Data Entry

The simplest way to enter data is by clicking on a cell and typing directly. Pressing **Enter** moves the selection down to the next row, while **Tab** moves it to the next column. Manual data entry is ideal for small datasets, but for larger ones, automation tools are more efficient.

2. Using Autofill for Faster Entry

Autofill is an efficient feature that automatically completes sequences, patterns, or repeated values.

Enter a starting value in a cell (e.g., "Monday").

Hover over the bottom-right corner of the cell until the **Fill Handle** (small plus sign) appears.

Drag the Fill Handle downward or sideways to continue the sequence.

Excel automatically recognizes common patterns such as days of the week, months, or numerical increments (e.g., 1, 2, 3, 4...).

3. Using Flash Fill for Pattern-Based Data Entry

Flash Fill detects and applies patterns without requiring formulas:

If your dataset includes structured text, enter an example of the desired format in a nearby column.

Press **Ctrl + E** after entering the first few examples, and Excel will recognize and complete the pattern.

This is particularly useful for splitting names, reformatting phone numbers, or extracting text from a dataset.

4. Copying and Pasting Data Efficiently

Excel allows various pasting options beyond the basic **Ctrl + C** (copy) and **Ctrl + V** (paste):

- **Paste Values:** Pastes only the numerical or text data, without formulas or formatting.
- **Paste Formatting:** Copies the formatting but not the actual data.
- **Paste Formulas:** Copies only the formula logic, applying it to the destination cells.
- **Paste Transpose:** Converts rows into columns and vice versa.

Right-click a cell and select **Paste Special** to choose from these options.

5. Data Validation to Control Input

Data validation helps maintain accuracy by restricting the type of values users can enter in specific cells. To set it up:

- Select the target cells.
- Go to **Data > Data Validation**.
- Choose criteria such as whole numbers, decimals, dates, or predefined lists.
- Set error messages to guide users if incorrect values are entered.

For example, if you want users to enter only dates in a specific range, setting a validation rule ensures that erroneous inputs are prevented.

6. Importing Data from External Sources

Instead of manually entering large datasets, you can import them:

- **CSV Files:** Open a .csv file directly in Excel.
- **Web Data:** Use **Data > Get Data > From Web** to extract information from online sources.
- **Databases:** Connect to databases via **Data > Get Data > From Database** for seamless integration.

Formatting Data for Clarity and Readability

Proper formatting enhances readability and ensures that your data is presented professionally. Excel offers numerous formatting tools to structure and emphasize important information.

1. Number Formatting

Numbers can be displayed in various formats:

- **General:** The default format with no special formatting.
- **Number:** Adds decimal places and thousands separators (e.g., 1,000.00).
- **Currency:** Displays monetary values with currency symbols (e.g., $1,250.50).
- **Percentage:** Converts decimals into percentages (e.g., $0.75 \rightarrow 75\%$).
- **Date/Time:** Formats numbers into readable dates and times.

To apply a format:

- Select the cells.
- Go to **Home** > **Number Format (dropdown menu)**.
- Choose the desired format.

2. Text Formatting for Readability

To improve text appearance, apply:

- Bold, Italics, Underline: Use the toolbar or shortcuts (Ctrl + B, Ctrl + I, Ctrl + U).
- Font Size and Color: Customize under Home > Font.
- Alignment: Adjust text position (left, center, right) under Home > Alignment.
- Wrap Text: Allows multi-line text within a cell.
- Merge & Center: Combines multiple cells into one for headers.

3. Using Borders and Shading to Organize Data

Borders and shading make tables more visually distinct:

- Add borders via **Home > Borders**.
- Apply shading using the **Fill Color** tool.

4. Conditional Formatting to Highlight Key Data

Conditional formatting dynamically changes cell appearance based on values:

- Select the target range.
- Go to **Home > Conditional Formatting**.
- Choose options like **Color Scales, Data Bars, or Icon Sets**.
- Set custom rules (e.g., highlight values above 100).

Enhancing Presentation with Themes and Styles

To create visually appealing and consistent spreadsheets, Excel offers themes and cell styles.

1. Applying a Theme for Consistency

Themes provide pre-set color and font combinations:

Go to Page **Layout > Themes**.

Select a built-in theme or create a custom one.

2. Using Cell Styles for Quick Formatting

Cell styles provide predefined formatting for headings, totals, and notes:

- Go to Home > Cell Styles.

- Apply a style to emphasize key data points.

3. Customizing Themes to Match Your Preferences

You can modify a theme by adjusting:

- **Fonts:** Select **Page Layout > Fonts** to change the typeface.
- **Colors:** Adjust under **Page Layout > Colors**.
- **Effects:** Modify visual elements via **Page Layout > Effects**.

To save your custom theme:

- Click **Page Layout > Themes > Save Current Theme**.
- Reuse it across multiple workbooks for consistency.

Conclusion

Understanding how to enter and format data effectively is a crucial skill in Excel. This chapter covered various data entry techniques, including

Autofill, Flash Fill, and Data Validation, along with formatting tools like number styles, text enhancements, and conditional formatting. By mastering these techniques, you can create organized, visually appealing, and error-free spreadsheets.

In the next chapter, we will explore **Basic Formulas and Functions**, where you'll learn how to perform calculations, automate tasks, and manipulate data efficiently.

Chapter 3: Basic Formulas and Functions

Microsoft Excel is a powerful tool for performing calculations, analyzing data, and making informed decisions. At its core, Excel's strength lies in its ability to process formulas and functions efficiently. Whether you are handling simple arithmetic or performing complex operations, understanding Excel's formula system is essential for maximizing productivity.

In this chapter, we will explore the fundamentals of Excel formulas, discuss commonly used functions such as SUM, AVERAGE, and IF, and learn how to troubleshoot errors in formulas. By the end of this chapter, you will be able to construct formulas confidently, apply essential functions, and resolve formula-related issues effectively.

Understanding Excel Formulas

What is a Formula?

A formula in Excel is an expression used to perform calculations on values within a worksheet. Every formula begins with an equal sign (=), followed by numbers, cell references, operators, and functions.

Basic Arithmetic Operations in Excel

Excel supports fundamental mathematical operations, making it easy to conduct calculations within your spreadsheet. Here are some basic operations:

- **Addition (+)**: =A1 + B1
- **Subtraction (-)**: =A1 - B1
- **Multiplication (*)**: =A1 * B1
- **Division (/)**: =A1 / B1
- **Exponentiation (^)**: =A1^B1

For example, if A1 contains 10 and B1 contains 5, using =A1 + B1 will result in 15.

Using Cell References in Formulas

Instead of entering numbers manually, it is more efficient to use cell references. Cell references allow formulas to update automatically when input values change, making calculations dynamic.

For instance,

rather than typing =10 + 20, it is preferable to write =A1 + B1. If the value in A1 changes, the formula updates accordingly without requiring manual intervention.

Order of Operations in Excel (PEMDAS)

Excel follows the standard mathematical order of operations, also known as **PEMDAS**:

1. **Parentheses** () – Operations inside parentheses are executed first.
2. **Exponents** ^ – Power calculations come next.
3. **Multiplication and Division** *, / – Processed from left to right.
4. **Addition and Subtraction** +, - – Processed last from left to right.

Example:

- =10 + 5 * 2 results in 20 because multiplication takes precedence.

- =(10 + 5) * 2 results in 30 because parentheses alter the order of operations.

Commonly Used Functions in Excel: SUM, AVERAGE, IF

What is a Function?

A function in Excel is a predefined formula designed to perform specific calculations. Functions simplify complex computations, improve efficiency, and reduce the chances of errors.

1. SUM Function (Adding Values)

The SUM function is used to add multiple values in a specified range.

Syntax:

=SUM(range)

Example: If cells A1 through A5 contain {5, 10, 15, 20, 25}, then:

=SUM(A1:A5)

returns 75.

2. AVERAGE Function (Calculating Mean)

The AVERAGE function calculates the mean value of a given range of numbers.

Syntax:

=AVERAGE(range)

Example: If A1 through A5 contain {10, 20, 30, 40, 50}, then:

=AVERAGE(A1:A5)

returns 30.

3. IF Function (Conditional Logic)

The IF function performs a logical test and returns different values based on whether the condition is met.

Syntax:

=IF(condition, value_if_true, value_if_false)

Example:

=IF(A1>50, "Pass", "Fail")

If A1 contains 60, the result will be **"Pass"**.

If A1 contains 40, the result will be **"Fail"**.

Handling Formula Errors in Excel

Errors in Excel can occur due to various reasons, such as incorrect references, invalid values, or syntax mistakes. Understanding these errors helps in troubleshooting and ensuring smooth calculations.

Common Excel Errors

Error Code	Meaning	How to Fix
#DIV/0!	Division by zero	Ensure the denominator is not zero. Use =IF(B1=0,

		"Error", A1/B1).
#VALUE!	Incorrect data type	Ensure the function receives the expected input type (e.g., numbers instead of text).
#REF!	Invalid cell reference	Avoid deleting referenced cells in formulas. Update references accordingly.
#NAME?	Undefined function or name	Check for typos in function names or

		ensure named ranges exist.
#NUM!	Invalid numerical value	Verify that numbers fall within acceptable ranges.

Using IFERROR to Handle Errors

To prevent disruptive errors, Excel provides the IFERROR function, which returns a custom message when an error occurs.

Syntax:

=IFERROR(expression, custom_message)

Example:

=IFERROR(A1/B1, "Invalid Calculation")

If B1 is zero, instead of displaying #DIV/0!, Excel will show **"Invalid Calculation"**.

Advanced Formula Techniques

Absolute and Relative Cell References

- Relative References: Change when copied to another location (A1 → B1).

- Absolute References: Do not change when copied (A1).

- Mixed References: Partially locked references (A$1 or $A1).

Example: If =A1*B1 is copied from row 1 to row 2, it updates to =A2*B2 (relative reference). If using =A1*B1, the reference to A1 remains fixed.

Concatenation (Joining Texts)

The & operator or CONCATENATE function joins text values.

Example:

=A1 & " " & B1

If A1 contains "John" and B1 contains "Doe", the result is **"John Doe"**.

Conclusion

Mastering Excel formulas and functions is essential for efficient data analysis and decision-making. By understanding arithmetic operations, leveraging commonly used functions, and handling errors effectively, you can work with spreadsheets confidently.

Chapter 4: Managing Worksheets in Excel

Excel workbooks typically contain multiple worksheets, each serving a distinct purpose in your data analysis or record-keeping. With larger workbooks, it's important to know how to efficiently manage these sheets. By mastering techniques for inserting, renaming, deleting, and linking sheets, you can enhance the structure and navigation of your Excel files, making it much easier to work with extensive datasets.

In this chapter, we'll explore:

- The essentials of inserting, deleting, and renaming worksheets
- How to create a Table of Contents with hyperlinks for smoother navigation
- Best practices for organizing worksheets to improve workflow efficiency

By the end of this chapter, you will be well-equipped to handle large Excel workbooks and navigate between multiple sheets with ease.

Inserting, Deleting, and Renaming Worksheets

Inserting a New Worksheet

Adding new worksheets in Excel is essential when you need to organize different sets of data within the same workbook. Excel provides several methods for inserting worksheets quickly and efficiently:

- **Method 1: Using the Plus Icon**
  If you're working within a workbook and need a new sheet, the quickest method is to click the plus (+) icon at the bottom of the window. This will insert a new worksheet, and Excel will automatically assign it a default name like "Sheet2".

- **Method 2: Using the Ribbon**
  For more options, go to the Home tab and

click on the "Insert" button, then select "Insert Sheet". This action also adds a new worksheet to your workbook.

- **Method 3: Keyboard Shortcut**
  A very efficient way to insert a new worksheet is by using the keyboard shortcut Shift + F11. This instantly adds a new worksheet to your workbook.

Deleting a Worksheet

There are times when you may need to remove a worksheet that is no longer necessary. Deleting a worksheet in Excel is a straightforward process, but it's important to be cautious, as the data will be lost once deleted.

Steps to Delete a Worksheet:

1. Right-click on the worksheet tab that you want to delete.
2. From the context menu, choose "Delete".

3. If the worksheet contains any data, Excel will ask you to confirm that you want to delete the sheet.

4. Click "OK" to complete the deletion.

Tip: Be careful when deleting sheets, as the process is irreversible. It's always wise to make a backup of important data before removing sheets.

Renaming a Worksheet

Renaming worksheets can make your workbook more organized and easier to navigate. By giving your sheets meaningful names, you can quickly identify their contents, which is especially useful when working with large Excel files.

Steps to Rename a Worksheet:

1. Double-click on the worksheet tab that you wish to rename.

2. Type the new name for the sheet.

3. Press "Enter" to confirm the change.

Alternatively, you can right-click the sheet tab, select "Rename", type the desired name, and press "Enter".

Tip: When naming your worksheets, avoid using special characters like /, *, ?, or : since Excel does not allow these characters in worksheet names.

Creating a Table of Contents with Hyperlinks

For workbooks with numerous sheets, having a Table of Contents (TOC) can save you significant time when navigating between sheets. By creating a TOC, you can use hyperlinks to quickly jump to any part of your workbook, enhancing your productivity.

Steps to Create a TOC with Hyperlinks:

1. **Insert a New Sheet**:
   First, insert a new worksheet at the beginning of your workbook and name it "Table of Contents". This sheet will act as a central hub for navigating your workbook.

2. **List the Sheet Names**:

In the first column of the TOC sheet (usually column A), type the names of all the sheets in your workbook. This gives you a clear, written outline of all the available sheets.

3. **Insert Hyperlinks**:

   - Select the cell where you want to create a hyperlink.
   - Press Ctrl + K or go to the "Insert" tab and click on "Hyperlink".
   - In the dialog box, select "Place in This Document".
   - A list of all the sheets in your workbook will appear. Choose the relevant sheet name, then click "OK".

4. **Test the Links**:

After creating the hyperlinks, it's important to test them. Click on each hyperlink in your TOC to ensure it takes you to the correct sheet.

Tip: To improve the look of your Table of Contents, you can format the text by using bold, changing font colors, or applying background colors to make it more visually appealing.

Organizing Worksheets for Efficiency

Reordering Worksheets

In larger workbooks, it's often necessary to change the order of your sheets to better suit the workflow. Excel allows you to easily rearrange sheets within a workbook.

Steps to Reorder Worksheets:

- Click and hold the tab of the worksheet you want to move.
- Drag the sheet to the desired position among the other sheets.
- Release the mouse button to drop the sheet in its new location.

Reordering sheets this way helps you group related information together, improving the structure and flow of your workbook.

Grouping and Ungrouping Worksheets

When working with multiple sheets that share the same formatting or need similar updates, grouping them together is a time-saving technique. Once grouped, any changes you make on one sheet will be applied to all grouped sheets simultaneously.

Steps to Group Worksheets:

1. Hold down the Ctrl key and click the tabs of the sheets you wish to group.
2. Any action you perform (e.g., entering data, formatting) on one of the grouped sheets will be mirrored across all the selected sheets.

To ungroup the sheets, simply click on a sheet that's not part of the group, and the grouping will be removed.

Tip: Grouping is especially helpful when applying consistent formatting across multiple sheets or when you need to input the same data across several sheets.

Coloring Worksheet Tabs

A quick way to visually distinguish between different types of data or sections within your workbook is to color code your worksheet tabs. This method enhances navigation and makes it easier to locate specific sheets at a glance.

Steps to Color Worksheet Tabs:
1. Right-click on the worksheet tab you want to color.
2. From the context menu, choose "Tab Color".
3. Select a color from the options provided.

Tip: Use color coding to represent different categories of data. For example, use blue for financial data, green for reports, and red for urgent tasks.

Freezing and Hiding Worksheets

Excel also provides features to help you manage your workbook's visibility and reduce clutter, such as freezing panes and hiding sheets.

Hiding Sheets: If certain sheets in your workbook are not frequently used, or if you want to temporarily conceal sensitive data, you can hide a sheet. This helps to declutter your workbook and makes it easier to focus on important sheets.

Steps to Hide a Sheet:

1. Right-click on the sheet tab.
2. Select "Hide" from the context menu.

To unhide a sheet, right-click on any sheet tab, select "Unhide", and choose the sheet you wish to reveal.

Freezing Panes: When working with large datasets, freezing rows or columns can be helpful to keep certain information visible while scrolling through the rest of the data.

Steps to Freeze Panes:

1. Select the row or column you want to freeze (e.g., the header row).
2. Go to the "View" tab and click on "Freeze Panes".
3. Select either "Freeze Top Row" or "Freeze First Column", depending on what you want to remain visible while scrolling.

Conclusion

Efficiently managing worksheets in Excel is a crucial skill, particularly when working with large workbooks that contain multiple sheets. By mastering techniques like inserting, renaming, and organizing worksheets, you can significantly improve your workflow and make navigating through your data much easier. Additionally, using features like Tables of Contents, grouping sheets, and color coding enhances the clarity and accessibility of your workbook.

Week 2: Data Visualization and Analysis

Chapter 5: Creating and Customizing Charts

Visualizing data effectively is a key skill in Excel. By transforming complex numbers into clear, graphical representations, you can quickly identify trends, patterns, and insights. Whether you're presenting data to a team or analyzing your own findings, charts are indispensable for simplifying data interpretation. This chapter will guide you on how to choose the right chart for your dataset, customize your charts for clarity, and leverage sparklines for quick, at-a-glance visual analysis.

In this chapter, we will cover:

- How to choose the right chart type for your data.

- Formatting and customizing charts to ensure they are visually appealing and easy to understand.

- Using sparklines to display trends within a single cell for quick visual analysis.

By mastering these skills, you will not only enhance your ability to present data but also improve your capacity to analyze information with greater efficiency.

Selecting the Right Chart Type

Excel provides a wide array of chart types, each tailored to different kinds of data visualization. The key to creating effective charts lies in understanding which chart type is most suitable for your particular dataset. Whether you're comparing categories, showing trends over time, or representing proportions, Excel offers a chart that can best communicate your data story.

Common Excel Chart Types:

1. **Column and Bar Charts:** These are ideal for comparing values across different categories. They allow for easy visualization of data

distributions and differences between categories.

- o **Use Case Example**: Comparing monthly sales figures for various products.

2. **Line Charts:** Line charts are perfect for illustrating trends over a continuous period. They show changes in data over time, making them excellent for time-series analysis.

   - o **Use Case Example**: Tracking revenue or stock prices over several months or years.

3. **Pie Charts:** Pie charts are used to show how a single category or value is divided into its constituent parts. The visual impact of pie charts is particularly strong when representing proportional data.

   - o **Use Case Example**: Displaying the market share of different products in a business.

4. **Scatter (XY) Charts:** Scatter plots help in understanding the relationship between two different variables. Each point in the scatter chart represents a data pair, making it easy to visualize correlations.

   o **Use Case Example**: Exploring the relationship between temperature and ice cream sales.

5. **Area Charts:** These are similar to line charts but with the area below the line shaded. Area charts emphasize the magnitude of values over time, and they are useful when showing cumulative data.

   o **Use Case Example**: Displaying cumulative revenue over a year.

6. **Combo Charts:** Combo charts combine two different chart types in one, which useful when you need to compare different sets of data in the same chart.

- o **Use Case Example**: Comparing actual vs. projected sales with a combination of bar and line charts.

How to Insert a Chart in Excel:

1. First, select the data you want to chart. This can be a range of cells, or it can include both rows and columns.

2. Next, navigate to the **Insert tab** on the Ribbon.

3. Choose the chart type you need from the Charts group. Excel will display a variety of options, from column and line charts to more advanced chart types like radar and stock charts.

4. After inserting the chart, you can format it by adding titles, adjusting axis labels, and modifying the chart design to suit your needs.

Tip: If you're unsure about which chart to use, the **Recommended Charts** button in the Insert tab provides Excel's suggestions based on your selected data.

Formatting and Customizing Charts

Once you've inserted a chart, Excel gives you several powerful tools to customize it and make it look professional. Customizing your chart is not only about making it visually appealing; it's about improving its readability and ensuring it clearly conveys the right message.

Adding Titles and Labels:

1. Click on the chart to activate the Chart Tools.
2. You'll notice a **Chart Elements** button (a plus sign) at the top-right corner of the chart.
3. Check the options for **Chart Title** and **Axis Titles** to make sure that the chart is well-labeled.
4. Customize these titles with meaningful descriptions of the data being displayed (e.g., "Monthly Sales" or "Revenue Growth").

Adjusting Colors and Styles:

1. Click on the chart to activate the **Chart Design** tab in the Ribbon.

2. Use the **Change Colors** button to adjust the color scheme of your chart, selecting a palette that enhances visibility and understanding.

3. Choose a predefined style from the **Chart Styles** gallery to further enhance your chart's aesthetic.

Modifying Data Series and Legends:

You can modify the appearance of the data series (bars, lines, or other elements) within your chart by right-clicking on them and selecting **Format Data Series**. This allows you to change the colors, patterns, or even the chart type for individual data series.

To modify the position of the **legend**, simply click on the legend and drag it to a preferred location on the chart.

Adding Data Labels:

Data labels are crucial for making your chart more informative. You can add them by:

1. Clicking on the chart to activate the Chart Elements.
2. Checking the **Data Labels** option.
3. Choosing where you want the labels to appear (e.g., inside or outside the bars, or at the top of the lines).

Changing Chart Types:

You may want to experiment with different chart types to find the one that best represents your data. To do so, right-click on the chart and select **Change Chart Type**. This gives you the flexibility to alter the chart type for a single data series or the entire chart.

Tip: Keep your color scheme simple and consistent, and avoid using too many chart styles that could make the chart cluttered or harder to interpret.

Using Sparklines for Data Trends

Sparklines are small, simple charts that fit within a single cell. They are ideal for quickly visualizing trends in a compact space, making them perfect for dashboards or quick data overviews.

Types of Sparklines:

1. **Line Sparklines** – These show trends over time and are most useful for time-series data.

2. **Column Sparklines** – These show individual data values and can be used to compare the relative magnitude of values in a series.

3. **Win/Loss Sparklines** – These are great for showing positive and negative changes in data over time, with wins represented by one color and losses by another.

How to Insert Sparklines:

1. Select an empty cell where you want the sparkline to appear.

2. Go to the **Insert tab** and choose **Sparklines**.

3. Select the range of data that you want to visualize with the sparkline.

4. Click **OK**, and the sparkline will be inserted into the selected cell.

Customizing Sparklines:

Once you've inserted a sparkline, Excel offers various customization options, including changing the colors of the sparkline and adding markers to highlight key points (like highs or lows). You can access these options through the **Sparkline Tools** tab that appears when the sparkline is selected.

Tip: Sparklines are especially useful for dashboards or summarizing data in a compact format. They provide a clear visual cue of trends without overwhelming the viewer.

Conclusion

Mastering charts and visualizations in Excel is a critical skill for anyone working with data. By selecting the right chart type, customizing your charts for clarity, and using sparklines to quickly visualize trends, you can create impactful and informative reports that help you and your audience make better decisions. Remember, the key is to choose the visualization method that best represents your data's story.

Chapter 6: Mastering Conditional Formatting

In the world of data analysis and presentation, being able to visualize trends, identify anomalies, and highlight key figures is crucial. Conditional Formatting in Excel is an indispensable tool that enables users to apply automatic formatting based on specific conditions. Whether you are aiming to emphasize critical values, highlight trends, or identify patterns, this feature allows you to make your data more accessible and insightful at a glance.

This chapter will guide you through:

- Understanding how to apply Conditional Formatting to reveal trends and patterns.
- Creating custom formatting rules to tailor your sheets to your exact needs.

- Leveraging powerful visual elements such as data bars, color scales, and icon sets to enhance the presentation of your data.

By the end of this chapter, you will have a deep understanding of how to use Conditional Formatting to make your spreadsheets not only visually appealing but also more insightful and user-friendly.

Understanding Conditional Formatting

Conditional Formatting is a feature that allows Excel to apply specific formats—such as color, font changes, or cell borders—based on the values or conditions within the data. It helps to quickly highlight trends, outliers, or other key data points that need attention.

One of the main advantages of using Conditional Formatting is that it automatically updates as your data changes. This dynamic feature allows for real-time visualization and ensures that your data presentation remains relevant, even as new values are entered.

How to Apply Conditional Formatting

Getting started with Conditional Formatting is simple, and the process can be tailored to suit the type of data you're working with. Here's how you can apply it:

1. **Select the Range of Data:**
   - Start by highlighting the cells that you want to apply the formatting to. You can select an entire column, row, or a specific range of cells.

2. **Access the Home Tab:**
   - Navigate to the **Home Tab** on the Ribbon, where you'll find the **Styles group**. Click on **Conditional Formatting** to open the drop-down menu.

3. **Choose a Rule Type:**
   - Excel offers a variety of built-in formatting rules. These include:

- **Highlight Cells Rules**: Great for highlighting specific values like those greater than or less than a certain threshold.
- **Top/Bottom Rules**: Ideal for showcasing the top 10% of values or the bottom performers.
- **Data Bars, Color Scales, Icon Sets**: For more graphical visualization of data.

You can also create **custom rules** that are tailored to your needs.

4. **Adjust the Formatting Options:**
    - After selecting your desired rule, you can customize the formatting style. Choose from a wide range of formatting options, such as font color, fill color, borders, and more.
5. **Click OK:**

- Once you've set the desired formatting, simply click **OK** to apply the rule. The changes will automatically update as your data changes.

Common Conditional Formatting Rules

There are several standard rules available in Excel to help highlight trends and key data points. Let's explore the most commonly used rules:

1. **Highlighting Values Greater Than or Less Than:**
   - For example, if you're working with sales figures and you want to highlight values above $10,000 in green and values below $5,000 in red, this rule will allow you to do so with ease.
   - This type of formatting makes it clear when values are above or below a set threshold, helping to instantly identify high or low values.

2. **Identifying Duplicates:**

- Excel can automatically highlight duplicate entries in a data set. This is particularly useful when working with large datasets to identify redundant entries that need to be reviewed or cleaned up.
- Example: In a customer database, you may want to flag duplicate email addresses to avoid sending multiple communications to the same person.

3. **Highlighting Blank Cells:**
   - It's often useful to flag empty cells to ensure that no important data is overlooked. By setting a rule to highlight blank cells, you can quickly identify which fields need to be populated.
   - Example: In an order form, any missing customer contact information can be immediately identified by applying a rule to highlight blank cells.

4. **Using Formulas in Conditional Formatting:**

   ○ Conditional Formatting can also work with formulas. By using a formula, you can create more complex, custom rules that go beyond the built-in options.

   ○ For instance, you could highlight all rows where sales fall below the average sales for the month by using a formula like:

```excel
=A2<AVERAGE(A:A)
```

Tip: Conditional Formatting is an excellent tool for creating interactive dashboards. It allows you to visualize trends and identify patterns quickly, making your data much more accessible.

Creating Custom Rules

While Excel's pre-defined rules are incredibly useful, sometimes you need more flexibility. Custom rules allow you to design specific formatting based on your needs, giving you greater control over the visual representation of your data.

How to Create a Custom Rule:

1. **Select the Data Range:**
   - Choose the range of cells that you want to apply the custom formatting to.

2. **Open the New Rule Dialog:**
   - Navigate to the **Home Tab** > **Conditional Formatting** > **New Rule**. This opens the **New Formatting Rule** dialog.

3. **Use a Formula:**
   - From the list of rule types, choose **Use a formula to determine which cells to format**. This gives you the ability to enter a formula that evaluates to TRUE or FALSE.

4. **Enter Your Formula:**
   - Enter the formula that defines your condition. For example, to highlight all

rows where a customer's order is overdue, use the following formula:

- =$D2<TODAY()

- This formula compares the date in column D with today's date, highlighting any rows where the order is overdue.

5. **Choose Your Formatting:**

   - Click the **Format** button to define the style of the formatting (e.g., font color, fill color, borders, etc.).

6. **Click OK:**

   - Once you've set up your rule and chosen the formatting, click **OK** to apply the custom rule.

Examples of Custom Rules

Here are a few examples of custom rules you can create in Excel:

1. **Highlighting Rows Based on Conditions:**

- o Suppose you want to color entire rows where a customer's order is overdue. Use the formula:

```excel
=$D2<TODAY()
```

- o This will format the entire row where the date in column D is earlier than the current date, signaling overdue orders.

2. **Highlighting Alternating Rows for Readability:**

- o A common technique for improving readability is to apply alternating row colors. This is especially useful in large tables with many entries.

```excel
=MOD(ROW(),2)=0
```

- o This formula applies the formatting to every second row, creating a striped effect for easier reading.

3. **Flagging Cells Containing Specific Text:**

- To highlight all cells that contain the word "Urgent," use the following formula:

```excel
=SEARCH("Urgent",A2)
```

- This rule will apply the specified formatting to any cell that contains the word "Urgent," making it stand out in the dataset.

Tip: Custom rules give you the flexibility to design complex, data-driven formatting that meets your exact needs, making your spreadsheets much more dynamic and interactive.

Using Data Bars, Color Scales, and Icon Sets

Excel provides additional visualization tools through Conditional Formatting, such as Data Bars, Color Scales, and Icon Sets. These tools help to present data visually in ways that are intuitive and easy to interpret.

Data Bars:

Data Bars are a visual tool that places a bar within each cell, with the length of the bar corresponding to the value within the cell. This makes it easy to compare values visually.

How to Apply Data Bars:

1. Select the data range you wish to format.
2. Click **Conditional Formatting** > **Data Bars**.
3. Choose either a **gradient fill** or a **solid fill** to apply the bars.

Example Usage:

- You could use Data Bars to represent sales performance, where higher sales have longer bars, giving an immediate visual comparison of performance across different regions or products.

Color Scales:

Color Scales apply a gradient of colors to your data, where each color represents a different value. This allows you to quickly see high, medium, and low values based on the color gradient.

How to Apply Color Scales:

1. Select the data range.
2. Click **Conditional Formatting** > **Color Scales**.
3. Choose a gradient color scheme (for example, red for low values, yellow for medium values, and green for high values).

Example Usage:

- Color Scales can be useful for visualizing temperature variations, where red represents high temperatures and blue represents low temperatures, making it easy to spot extreme values.

Icon Sets:

Icon Sets add small images or icons to your cells, such as arrows, flags, or traffic lights. These icons help you visualize trends, performance, and other data attributes at a glance.

How to Apply Icon Sets:

1. Select the range of data.
2. Click **Conditional Formatting** > **Icon Sets**.
3. Choose an icon set style (e.g., traffic lights, arrows, or check marks).

Example Usage:

- Icon sets are great for displaying stock price movement. For example, a green up arrow might indicate a price increase, a yellow right arrow for no change, and a red down arrow for a decrease.

Tip: Icon sets are an excellent way to provide a visual summary of your data, allowing for quick analysis without having to interpret the raw numbers.

Managing and Removing Conditional Formatting

Over time, your spreadsheet may accumulate multiple formatting rules. Excel provides tools to help you manage and remove these rules when necessary.

Editing a Conditional Formatting Rule:

To modify an existing rule, follow these steps:

1. Select the cells with the formatting you want to change.
2. Click on **Conditional Formatting** > **Manage Rules**.
3. Choose the rule you want to modify and click **Edit Rule**.
4. Adjust the conditions and formatting style as needed.

Removing Conditional Formatting:

If you no longer need a particular formatting rule, Excel makes it easy to remove:

1. Select the cells with the formatting.

2. Go to **Conditional Formatting** > **Clear Rules**.

3. You can choose to **Clear Rules from Selected Cells** or **Clear Rules from Entire Sheet**, depending on your needs.

Tip: Keep your formatting rules organized to prevent conflicts between multiple rules. Regularly review your rules to ensure they are still relevant.

Conclusion

Conditional Formatting is a powerful feature that can turn a basic spreadsheet into an insightful, visually engaging tool. By highlighting important data points, applying custom rules, and utilizing visual aids such as Data Bars and Icon Sets, you can create a dynamic and interactive data presentation. Whether you're analyzing sales trends, tracking project milestones, or simply improving data readability, mastering Conditional Formatting will take your Excel skills to the next level.

Chapter 7: Sorting and Filtering Data

Efficient data organization is essential when working with large datasets, and two key techniques that can significantly enhance your data analysis in Excel are sorting and filtering. Sorting allows you to arrange data in a structured order, making it easier to identify trends and draw insights. Filtering, on the other hand, enables you to narrow down the dataset to focus on specific data points, simplifying the decision-making process.

This chapter will guide you through both basic and advanced sorting techniques, show you how to use filters to analyze data more effectively, and demonstrate how to remove duplicates and validate data to ensure accuracy.

By mastering these techniques, you will be able to manage and interpret your data efficiently, ensuring that your analysis is not only accurate but also insightful.

Sorting Techniques: Basic and Advanced Methods

Sorting in Excel is a straightforward yet powerful tool that helps in organizing your data in a manner that is easy to understand and analyze. Whether you are sorting by a single column or applying multiple criteria, Excel offers a range of sorting options that cater to various needs.

Basic Sorting

Basic sorting involves ordering data in ascending or descending order based on the values in a selected column. Here's how you can quickly apply basic sorting:

1. **Select the Data Range**
   - Click anywhere within the dataset, ensuring that you have selected the entire range of data that you wish to sort.

2. **Open the Sort Menu**

   ○ Navigate to the **Data** tab in the Excel ribbon, then click on the **Sort** button.

3. **Choose Sorting Criteria**

   ○ A dialog box will appear. From here, you can select the column that you want to sort by. You can then choose whether to sort the data in **Ascending** order (A-Z or smallest to largest) or **Descending** order (Z-A or largest to smallest).

4. **Apply Sorting**

   ○ Click **OK** to apply the sorting, and Excel will automatically rearrange your data based on the selected criteria.

This simple method is ideal when you are working with a smaller dataset or need to organize your data based on a single column.

Advanced Sorting

Advanced sorting allows you to organize your data based on multiple columns, enabling a more nuanced analysis. Here's how you can apply advanced sorting:

1. **Open the Sort Menu**
   - Click **Data** > **Sort** to open the Sort dialog box.

2. **Add Sorting Levels**
   - In the dialog box, click on the **Add Level** button to introduce multiple levels of sorting. For instance, you may want to first sort by Region and then by Sales Amount.

3. **Select the Sorting Order**
   - For each column you add, you can specify whether to sort in **Ascending** or **Descending** order.

4. **Click OK**
   - Once you have added all the levels and specified the desired order, click **OK**, and Excel will apply your custom sorting preferences.

Tip: Excel also allows you to create custom lists to sort non-alphabetical data (such as months or days of the week) in the correct order.

Filtering Data to Focus on Specific Information

Filters in Excel are incredibly useful for narrowing down data and focusing on specific subsets based on criteria that are important to your analysis. Using filters allows you to hide irrelevant rows temporarily, making it easier to focus on the most relevant data points.

How to Apply Filters

1. **Select the Data Range**
   - Click anywhere inside the dataset to make it active.
2. **Enable Filters**
   - Go to the **Data** tab and click on **Filter**. This will add a drop-down arrow to the headers of each column.
3. **Filter by Criteria**

o Click the drop-down arrow in the header of the column you wish to filter. You can select various options based on the type of data in the column:

- **Text Filters**: For example, you can filter for cells that "contain" a specific word or "do not contain" a particular phrase.

- **Number Filters**: Options such as "greater than," "less than," or "equal to" allow you to filter based on numeric data.

- **Date Filters**: You can filter dates by a range (e.g., "this month," "last year," or a custom range).

4. **View Filtered Results**

o Once you've applied the filter, Excel will hide any rows that do not match your criteria, displaying only the data that meets your specifications.

Filters are dynamic, meaning you can quickly adjust them as you work with your data without permanently altering the underlying dataset.

Advanced Filtering for More Complex Criteria

For more sophisticated filtering needs, Excel's Advanced Filter option provides greater flexibility. Here's how you can use it:

1. **Navigate to Advanced Filter**
   - Go to **Data > Advanced** to open the Advanced Filter dialog box.
2. **Set the Criteria Range**
   - Define a criteria range that includes the conditions you want to apply. For example, if you want to filter for sales greater than $5,000, you would specify that as your condition in a separate range.
3. **Copy Results to Another Location (Optional)**

- If you want to keep the original data intact, you can choose to copy the filtered results to a different location.

4. **Click OK**
   - Click **OK** to apply the filter, and Excel will display only the rows that meet your criteria.

Tip: Filters are a great way to segment data dynamically and perform a deep analysis without affecting your original dataset.

Removing Duplicates and Ensuring Data Accuracy

When working with large datasets, duplicates can often sneak in, leading to skewed results and errors in your analysis. Excel provides an easy way to remove duplicates and ensure that your dataset is clean and accurate.

How to Remove Duplicates

1. **Select the Data Range**

o Highlight the columns where you suspect duplicates may exist.

2. **Open the Remove Duplicates Tool**

   o Click **Data > Remove Duplicates** to open the Remove Duplicates dialog box.

3. **Choose Columns to Check**

   o Select the specific columns where duplicates should be identified. For example, if you're checking for duplicate email addresses, select the column that contains those addresses.

4. **Click OK**

   o Once you've selected the columns, click **OK**, and Excel will remove any duplicate entries, leaving only unique records.

Data Validation to Ensure Accuracy

Data validation is another powerful tool in Excel that ensures only valid data is entered into your cells. It helps reduce errors by enforcing rules on the types of data users can input.

1. **Select the Cells to Validate**
   - Highlight the range where you want to apply validation rules.

2. **Open the Data Validation Tool**
   - Click **Data > Data Validation** to open the Data Validation dialog box.

3. **Choose Validation Criteria**
   - You can define various validation criteria:
     - Allow only whole numbers between a specified range.
     - Restrict input to a predefined list (e.g., Yes/No, specific departments, etc.).

4. **Set Input Messages and Error Alerts**
   - Add an input message that guides users on what type of data is acceptable. You can also set up error alerts that inform users if they attempt to enter invalid data.

5. **Click OK**

- Once you have set up the validation, click **OK**, and the validation rules will be applied to the selected cells.

Tip: Use data validation to ensure that all users enter accurate and consistent information, which is especially important for collaborative work.

Conclusion

Sorting and filtering are powerful tools that allow you to manage and analyze large datasets with ease. By mastering these techniques, you can quickly identify trends, clean up your data, and ensure that your analysis is based on accurate and relevant information.

In addition, removing duplicates and applying data validation rules will help maintain the integrity of your data, ensuring that your insights are based on reliable information.

Chapter 8: Introduction to PivotTables

PivotTables in Excel are incredibly powerful tools that allow you to quickly summarize, analyze, and visualize large datasets. Whether you're dealing with sales figures, customer feedback, financial reports, or any other type of data, PivotTables provide an intuitive way to extract valuable insights. These tools enable you to arrange and filter data dynamically, without altering the underlying dataset.

Mastering PivotTables can make your data analysis significantly more efficient, as they allow you to organize complex datasets in ways that make sense to you. With just a few clicks, you can turn raw data into meaningful summaries, helping you make informed business decisions or gain insights into key performance indicators.

In this chapter, we'll guide you through the following essential skills related to PivotTables:

- Creating PivotTables from Raw Data
- Customizing PivotTable Layouts
- Using Slicers and Timelines to Filter Data

By the end of this chapter, you'll be equipped to create and customize PivotTables, making your data analysis much more powerful and flexible.

Creating PivotTables from Raw Data

One of the biggest advantages of using PivotTables is their ability to take large amounts of unorganized data and turn it into a manageable, summarized format. Instead of scrolling through hundreds or thousands of rows, a PivotTable can give you a snapshot of the information you need, such as totals, averages, or specific data comparisons.

Steps to Create a PivotTable

1. **Ensure Your Data is Well-Structured**

   Before creating a PivotTable, it's essential that

your data is organized in a clean and structured manner. Your data should be in a tabular format, with clear headers for each column and no blank rows or columns in the middle of your dataset. Each column should contain only one type of data (e.g., dates, numbers, text).

2. **Select Your Data Range**

   o Begin by clicking anywhere within your dataset. If your data is in a table format, Excel will automatically select the entire table. If your data is not in a table format, you may need to manually select the range of cells you wish to include in the PivotTable.

3. **Insert the PivotTable**

   o Navigate to the **Insert** tab in the Excel ribbon.

   o Click on the **PivotTable** button. Excel will prompt you to select the range of data you want to analyze. If your data is already in a table format, this step is automatic.

- You will then be asked whether you want to place the PivotTable in a new worksheet or an existing one. Generally, it's recommended to choose a **New Worksheet** for clarity.

- After selecting your desired placement, click **OK**.

4. **Building the PivotTable**

- Once you click OK, a blank PivotTable will be created, and the **PivotTable Field List** will appear on the right-hand side of your screen. This is where the magic happens. The fields listed here correspond to the headers in your original dataset.

- To build your PivotTable, you need to drag the fields into the correct sections:

  - **Rows**: This is where you drag the fields that define the main categories (e.g., Product Names, Regions, or Customer IDs).

- **Columns**: This section is used for the fields that define comparison categories (e.g., Years, Months, or Product Types).

- **Values**: This is where numerical data (like sales, revenue, or quantities) goes. The PivotTable will calculate and summarize the data based on your selection (e.g., sum, average).

- **Filters**: Filters allow you to narrow down your data further. For instance, if you want to filter by specific regions or sales representatives, you can place those fields in the Filters section.

5. **Analyzing Your Data**
   o After constructing your PivotTable, you can adjust it to further analyze the data.

You can move fields around to change how the data is grouped or filtered, sort values to find the highest or lowest numbers, or apply different summarizing techniques (like averaging or counting). As you change the layout or data fields, the PivotTable updates automatically.

Tip: Excel has a feature called **Recommended PivotTables**. By selecting your dataset and choosing **Insert > Recommended PivotTables**, Excel will suggest several ways to visualize your data based on your dataset's characteristics. This is a great way to get started if you're unsure how to organize your data.

Customizing PivotTable Layouts

Although a PivotTable automatically generates a basic summary report, customizing it can improve readability, provide more insights, and make it easier to share with others.

Modifying the Report Layout

1. **Change the Layout Style**
   - Click anywhere within the PivotTable.
   - Go to the **PivotTable Design** tab.
   - Under the **Layout** section, you'll see several options for changing the way the PivotTable looks:
     - **Compact Form** (default): This is the most condensed view, where fields are grouped into a single column.
     - **Outline Form**: This layout adds more space between rows and columns, making it easier to read.
     - **Tabular Form**: This is great for copying and pasting PivotTables into other reports, as it displays the data in a more conventional table format.
2. **Rearranging Fields**
   - You can change the arrangement of rows and columns by dragging fields in the

PivotTable Field List. For instance, moving a product category from the Rows section to the Columns section will give you a new perspective on your data.

3. **Grouping Data**

   - To analyze data by specific time periods or categories, right-click on any field in the PivotTable and choose **Group**. For example, if you have a list of dates, you can group them into months, quarters, or years, making it easier to track trends over time.

   - Grouping can also be applied to numerical data. For instance, if you're analyzing sales figures, you can group them into ranges (e.g., $0-$100, $101-$500, etc.).

4. **Summarizing Values**

   - By default, Excel will sum the numerical data in the **Values** section. However, you can change the type of calculation by clicking on the dropdown next to a value and selecting **Value Field Settings**.

- Excel offers various summary functions, including:
    - **Sum**: Adds up all the values.
    - **Average**: Computes the average of the values.
    - **Count**: Counts the number of entries.
    - **Max/Min**: Shows the highest or lowest values.
    - **Percentage**: Shows data as a percentage of the total.

5. **Applying Number Formatting**

- If you want your PivotTable to display numbers in a specific format, right-click a value and choose **Number Format**. You can apply formats such as currency, percentage, or date format to make your data more readable and consistent.

Tip: Use **Conditional Formatting** to visually highlight data trends. For example, you could highlight the highest and lowest sales figures using color scales or data bars to make key information stand out.

Using Slicers and Timelines for Filtering

Slicers and timelines are interactive filtering tools that allow you to filter data within PivotTables in a more visual and intuitive way. These tools can help you focus on specific data points without permanently altering the underlying dataset.

Adding Slicers

Slicers are visual filters that appear as buttons, allowing you to quickly select and filter data in a PivotTable. They provide a more interactive experience compared to traditional filters.

1. **Insert a Slicer**
   - Click anywhere inside the PivotTable.

- Go to the **Insert** tab and click on **Slicer**.
- In the dialog box, select the field(s) you want to filter by (e.g., Region, Product Category).
- Click **OK**, and the slicer will appear as a floating panel on the screen.

2. **Use the Slicer to Filter Data**

- Click on the buttons in the slicer to filter the PivotTable data based on your selection. For example, you can click on "North America" in the Region slicer to display data only for that region.
- You can also select multiple items within a slicer by holding the **Ctrl** key or selecting a range of items by clicking and dragging.

Tip: Slicers can be formatted using the **Slicer Tools** tab. You can change the color, layout, and style of the slicer to match your report's design.

Adding Timelines

A **Timeline** is a specialized slicer for date fields. It allows you to filter your PivotTable based on time periods, such as years, months, quarters, or even specific dates.

1. **Insert a Timeline**
   - Click anywhere in the PivotTable.
   - Go to the **Insert** tab and select **Timeline**.
   - Choose a date field (e.g., Order Date) from your data.
   - Click **OK**, and a timeline slider will appear at the top of your PivotTable.
2. **Use the Timeline to Filter Data**
   - Use the slider to filter your data by specific time periods. For example, you can slide the bar to display data from the first quarter of the year or from a specific month.

Tip: Timelines make it easy to track trends and patterns over time without manually adjusting filters. They're especially useful when analyzing data over long periods, such as annual sales trends or quarterly performance.

Best Practices for Working with PivotTables

To get the most out of PivotTables, here are some essential best practices to keep in mind:

1. **Keep Your Data Clean**
   - Make sure there are no blank rows or columns in your dataset. Consistent formatting (such as using the same date or number format) will also make the PivotTable creation process smoother.

2. **Refresh Your Data**
   - If your dataset changes, make sure to refresh the PivotTable. You can do this by selecting the PivotTable and clicking **Refresh All** in the **PivotTable Analyze** tab.

3. **Use Multiple PivotTables**

- If you're working with large datasets, avoid cluttering a single PivotTable with too many fields. Instead, create multiple PivotTables that focus on different aspects of the data.

4. **Save PivotTable Templates**
   - If you frequently use similar PivotTable layouts, save your settings as a template so you can quickly apply them to new datasets.

5. **Avoid Overloading PivotTables**
   - Too many calculated fields or complex data models can slow down PivotTable performance. For very large datasets, consider using **Power Pivot** for enhanced data modeling capabilities.

Conclusion

PivotTables are an essential tool for summarizing, analyzing, and interpreting large datasets. They allow you to convert raw data into meaningful insights without altering the original dataset. By mastering the steps to create PivotTables, customizing their layout, and using slicers and timelines, you can gain deeper insights and present your findings in a clear and professional manner.

Week 3: Advanced Data Analysis

Chapter 9: Advanced Functions and Formulas in Excel

Microsoft Excel is a powerful tool used to analyze, manipulate, and visualize data. It serves as a cornerstone of many workplaces, especially in roles that require data analysis or reporting. As users progress from basic spreadsheet functions to more advanced capabilities, mastering advanced functions and formulas can significantly increase your efficiency and analytical power.

Advanced Excel functions allow users to perform sophisticated data manipulation, automate repetitive tasks, and extract insights from complex datasets that might otherwise be difficult to manage manually.

In this chapter, we will explore some of the most important advanced Excel functions, including:

- Lookup functions such as VLOOKUP, HLOOKUP, and the newly introduced XLOOKUP.
- Text functions like CONCATENATE, TEXTJOIN, and others used to combine and manipulate textual data.
- Logical functions such as AND, OR, and NOT that allow for decision-making in formulas.

Each of these functions plays a crucial role in enhancing your ability to work with large datasets, automate tasks, and solve complex problems. By the end of this chapter, you will be familiar with how to use these advanced functions and apply them to everyday work in Excel.

Lookup Functions: VLOOKUP, HLOOKUP, and XLOOKUP

One of the core features of Excel is its ability to look up and retrieve specific data from large tables or ranges. Lookup functions, such as VLOOKUP, HLOOKUP, and XLOOKUP, are invaluable when dealing with datasets that require searching and extracting values based on certain criteria.

VLOOKUP (Vertical Lookup)

The VLOOKUP function is one of the most commonly used lookup functions in Excel. It allows you to search for a value in the first column of a data range and retrieve the corresponding value from a specified column in the same row. VLOOKUP is best used when the data is organized in columns and you need to pull specific information from a table.

Syntax:

```pgsql
=VLOOKUP(lookup_value, table_array, col_index_num, [range_lookup])
```

- **lookup_value**: This is the value you are searching for.
- **table_array**: This is the range of cells that contains the data you want to search through.

- **col_index_num**: The column number within the table from which to retrieve the value.
- **[range_lookup]**: This optional argument determines whether you want an exact match (FALSE) or an approximate match (TRUE).

Example: Imagine you have a list of employees in columns A (Employee ID) and B (Employee Name). To retrieve the name of the employee with ID 105, you would use the following formula:

```php
=VLOOKUP(105, A2:B10, 2, FALSE)
```

This formula searches for employee ID 105 in column A and returns the corresponding name from column B.

Limitation of VLOOKUP: One major limitation of VLOOKUP is that it only searches from left to right. The value you want to search for must always be in the first column of your data range, which can make it less flexible in certain scenarios.

HLOOKUP (Horizontal Lookup)

HLOOKUP works similarly to VLOOKUP but searches for data horizontally across rows rather than vertically down columns. This function is useful when your data is organized in rows rather than columns, and you need to extract data from different rows.

Syntax:

```pgsql
=HLOOKUP(lookup_value, table_array, row_index_num, [range_lookup])
```

- **lookup_value**: The value you are searching for.
- **table_array**: The range where you want to search for the lookup value.
- **row_index_num**: The row number from which to return the value.
- **[range_lookup]**: Optional; can be TRUE for an approximate match or FALSE for an exact match.

Example: Let's say your product names are listed in row 1, and their corresponding sales figures are in row 2. To find the sales for "Product A," you can use the following formula:

```php
=HLOOKUP("Product A", A1:D2, 2, FALSE)
```

This formula will return the sales data from the second row corresponding to "Product A."

XLOOKUP (The Enhanced Lookup Function)

XLOOKUP is the most recent addition to Excel's lookup functions and is designed to replace both VLOOKUP and HLOOKUP. It offers more flexibility and power by allowing users to search for a value in any direction (left to right, right to left, top to bottom, or bottom to top) and eliminate some of the limitations found in older lookup functions.

Syntax:

```
=XLOOKUP(lookup_value, lookup_array, return_array, [if_not_found], [match_mode], [search_mode])
```

- **lookup_value**: The value to search for.
- **lookup_array**: The array or range containing the values you want to search through.
- **return_array**: The array or range containing the values you want to retrieve.
- **[if_not_found]**: Optional; what to return if the lookup value is not found.
- **[match_mode]**: Optional; defines whether you are looking for an exact match (0), an approximate match (1), or a wildcard match (2).
- **[search_mode]**: Optional; defines the direction of the search (start from the first or last entry).

Example: To find the name of an employee based on their ID from a list, you could use the following XLOOKUP formula:

```php
=XLOOKUP(105, A2:A10, B2:B10, "Not Found")
```

This formula searches for the value 105 in the range A2:A10 and returns the corresponding employee name from range B2:B10. If no match is found, it returns "Not Found."

Text Functions: CONCATENATE, TEXTJOIN, and More

Excel offers a variety of text functions to combine, manipulate, and format text data. These functions are essential for handling datasets that contain textual information such as names, addresses, or descriptions. Text functions allow you to join multiple strings together, extract specific characters, and format text for display.

CONCATENATE (or CONCAT in Newer Versions)

The CONCATENATE function allows you to join multiple text strings together into one. Although Excel has replaced CONCATENATE with CONCAT in newer versions, it remains widely used.

Syntax:

```
=CONCATENATE(text1, text2, ...)
```

- **text1, text2, ...:** These are the text strings or cell references that you want to join together.

Example: To combine "Hello" and "World" with a space between them, use the following formula:

```arduino
=CONCATENATE("Hello", " ", "World")
```

The result will be "Hello World."

Note: If you're using a newer version of Excel, consider using the CONCAT function instead, as it offers improved performance.

TEXTJOIN (A More Flexible Way to Combine Text)

TEXTJOIN is an advanced version of CONCATENATE that allows you to specify a delimiter (such as a space, comma, or hyphen) to separate the text strings. It also has the ability to ignore empty cells, making it much more versatile than CONCATENATE.

Syntax:

```
=TEXTJOIN(delimiter, ignore_empty, text1, text2, ...)
```

- **delimiter**: The separator between the text strings (e.g., a space, comma, or semicolon).
- **ignore_empty**: A Boolean value (TRUE or FALSE) that specifies whether to ignore empty cells.
- **text1, text2, ...:** The text strings or cell references that you want to join.

Example: To combine values from cells A2 to A5 with a comma and a space, and to ignore any empty cells, use the following formula:

```php
=TEXTJOIN(", ", TRUE, A2:A5)
```

This will join the values from cells A2 to A5, separated by commas, and exclude any empty cells from the result.

Logical Functions: AND, OR, and NOT

Logical functions are used to test conditions and return TRUE or FALSE based on the results. These functions are crucial for decision-making, especially when used within other formulas like IF statements.

AND Function

The AND function checks whether all given conditions are TRUE. It returns TRUE only if all conditions are met.

Syntax:

```
=AND(condition1, condition2, ...)
```

- **condition1, condition2, ...:** The conditions you want to test.

Example: If you want to check whether both values in cells A2 and B2 are greater than 50, you can use the following formula:

```
=AND(A2>50, B2<100)
```

This formula will return TRUE if both A2 and B2 are greater than 50; otherwise, it will return FALSE.

OR Function

The OR function returns TRUE if at least one of the conditions is TRUE. It is useful when you want to check if any of several conditions are met.

Syntax:

```
=OR(condition1, condition2, ...)
```

Example: If you want to check if either cell A2 or B2 contains a value greater than 50, use the following formula:

```
=OR(A2>50, B2<100)
```

This formula will return TRUE if either A2 or B2 is greater than 50.

NOT Function

The NOT function reverses the logical value of a given condition. If the condition is TRUE, NOT will return FALSE, and if the condition is FALSE, NOT will return TRUE.

Syntax:

```sql
=NOT(condition)
```

Example: To check if the value in A2 is NOT greater than 50, use the following formula:

```
=NOT(A2>50)
```

This will return TRUE if A2 is not greater than 50 and FALSE if A2 is greater than 50.

Conclusion

Mastering advanced Excel functions like VLOOKUP, HLOOKUP, XLOOKUP, CONCATENATE, TEXTJOIN, AND, OR, and NOT will not only increase your proficiency but will also help you work more efficiently and effectively. These functions unlock the ability to solve complex data problems, streamline your workflows, and make better data-driven decisions. As you continue to explore Excel, remember that these advanced formulas are just the beginning—there are countless other functions to learn that will enhance your skills even further.

Chapter 10: Data Validation and Protection

Excel is much more than a simple tool for organizing and analyzing data; it's also a robust platform designed to ensure the integrity and security of your information. Whether you're managing sensitive business data, creating financial reports, or maintaining databases, safeguarding the accuracy, consistency, and privacy of your work is paramount. Excel provides a variety of features to maintain data integrity, validate entries, and protect against unauthorized changes.

In this chapter, we will explore the following key areas of Excel's data validation and protection tools:

- How to set up and apply data validation rules.
- Methods for protecting worksheets and workbooks from accidental or unauthorized modifications.

- How to share workbooks and collaborate in real time while maintaining control over data security.

By the end of this chapter, you'll have acquired the necessary skills to protect your Excel documents and ensure the accuracy and security of the data within them.

Setting Data Validation Rules

Data validation in Excel helps maintain the quality of the data entered into your spreadsheets. This feature enables you to define rules and conditions that restrict or guide the kind of data users can input. Whether you're building a form, creating a budget, or tracking inventory, you can use data validation to prevent errors that could affect the integrity of your data. By enforcing specific rules, Excel ensures that only accurate, valid data is entered into your cells.

Applying Data Validation
Step-by-step guide:

1. **Select the Cells for Validation:**
   - The first step is to highlight the range of cells where you want to apply data validation. For example, you might want to restrict data entry in a column that contains dates, or only allow numeric entries in a cell where quantities are being tracked.

2. **Open the Data Validation Menu:**
   - Navigate to the **Data** tab on the Ribbon, and click on **Data Validation** in the **Data Tools** group. This opens the Data Validation dialog box, where you can define your rules.

3. **Choose a Validation Rule:**
   - In the **Data Validation** dialog box, the first option is to select a validation type from the drop-down list under **Allow**. The available options include numbers, dates, lists, and custom formulas.

4. **Set the Validation Criteria:**

- After selecting the validation type, you'll define the criteria. For example, if you're allowing only whole numbers between 1 and 100, set the range from 1 to 100.

5. **Customize the Input Message and Error Alert:**
   - Excel gives you the option to provide users with guidance through an **Input Message**. This message will appear when a user selects a cell, explaining what type of data is expected. Additionally, you can set up an **Error Alert** that pops up if invalid data is entered, notifying the user of the issue.

6. **Click OK to Apply the Validation:**
   - After setting up the validation rules, click **OK** to enforce the rules on the selected range.

Common Data Validation Rules

- **Restricting Numeric Entries:**

- If you're managing a budget or tracking quantities, you might need to restrict data entry to specific numbers. For example, if you want to limit entries to whole numbers between 1 and 100, select **Whole Number** from the **Allow** menu and set the appropriate range.

- **Creating Drop-down Lists:**
  - When you want users to select from predefined options, creating a drop-down list is an excellent approach. For example, you can create a drop-down list of color options (Red, Blue, Green). To do this, select **List** under **Allow**, and in the **Source** field, enter the available options separated by commas.

- **Setting Date Constraints:**
  - If you need to ensure users enter dates within a specific range, select **Date** under **Allow**, and then specify the start

and end dates. This ensures that the dates entered fall within the valid range.

- **Custom Formulas for Validation:**
  - ○ You can create more advanced rules by using custom formulas. For example, you might want to ensure that entered values are always positive. To do this, select **Custom** under **Allow** and enter the formula =A1>0 in the formula field.

Tip: Use the **Circle Invalid Data** feature to quickly highlight cells with invalid entries, allowing you to identify and correct issues easily.

Protecting Worksheets and Workbooks

Once you've set up your data validation rules, protecting your worksheets and workbooks becomes crucial for preventing accidental or unauthorized changes. Excel provides several methods for locking cells, protecting data, and securing the entire workbook.

Protecting a Worksheet

Excel allows you to protect individual worksheets by restricting the ability to edit cells or make changes to specific elements within the sheet. This is particularly useful when working with shared documents or protecting formulas.

Steps to Protect a Worksheet:

1. **Select the Cells to Lock or Unlock:**
   - By default, all cells in a worksheet are locked when protection is applied. However, you can unlock specific cells to allow users to make changes. Select the cells you want to leave unlocked, right-click, and choose **Format Cells**. Under the **Protection** tab, uncheck **Locked**.

2. **Enable Worksheet Protection:**
   - Once the desired cells are unlocked, go to the **Review** tab on the Ribbon and click **Protect Sheet**. This will open the **Protect Sheet** dialog box.

3. **Set a Password (Optional):**

o You can set a password to restrict access to the protected sheet. Users will need to enter the password to make changes to the protected worksheet.

4. **Choose Protection Options:**

o In the **Protect Sheet** dialog box, you can select various options for what users can and cannot do. You might allow users to format cells, insert rows, or sort data, or you can restrict all actions.

5. **Click OK to Apply Protection:**

o After selecting your desired options, click **OK** to apply the protection. Your worksheet is now secure from unauthorized changes.

Protecting a Workbook

In addition to protecting individual worksheets, you can protect the entire workbook. This prevents changes to the workbook's structure, such as adding, deleting, or moving sheets.

Steps to Protect a Workbook:

1. **Enable Workbook Protection:**

   o Go to the **Review** tab and click **Protect Workbook**. This opens the **Protect Workbook** dialog box.

2. **Choose Protection Type:**

   o You can choose to protect the **Structure** of the workbook, which prevents users from adding, deleting, or moving sheets. Alternatively, you can protect the **Windows**, which restricts users from resizing the workbook window.

3. **Set a Password (Optional):**

   o You can add an extra layer of security by setting a password. Without the password, users cannot make changes to the workbook structure.

4. **Click OK to Apply Protection:**

   o Once you've selected your protection options, click **OK** to enforce the protection on the workbook.

Encrypting a Workbook with a Password

For full security, especially if your workbook contains sensitive information, you can encrypt the entire workbook with a password. This ensures that only authorized users can open the file.

Steps to Encrypt a Workbook:

1. Click on **File** > **Info** > **Protect Workbook**.
2. Select **Encrypt with Password**.
3. Enter your desired password and confirm it.
4. Click **OK** to encrypt the workbook.

Warning: If you forget your password, you will not be able to recover or access the workbook, so it's essential to store your password securely.

Sharing and Collaborating on Workbooks

One of the greatest advantages of Excel is its ability to facilitate collaboration. With cloud-based tools like **OneDrive** and **SharePoint**, multiple users can work on a workbook simultaneously, which is particularly useful for teams or businesses that need to share data and make real-time updates.

Sharing a Workbook in OneDrive or SharePoint

1. **Save the Workbook to OneDrive or SharePoint:**
   - First, save your workbook to **OneDrive** or **SharePoint** by going to **File** > **Save As** and selecting the appropriate cloud storage location.

2. **Click the Share Button:**
   - Once the workbook is saved to the cloud, click the **Share** button in the top-right corner of the Excel window.

3. **Enter Email Addresses:**
   - In the **Share** dialog box, enter the email addresses of the people you want to share the workbook with. You can choose whether to allow them to **Edit** or only **View** the workbook.

4. **Click Send to Share the Workbook:**
   - After setting the permissions, click **Send** to send an email invitation to your

collaborators. They can now access and edit the workbook in real-time.

Enabling Track Changes

When collaborating with others, it's important to track changes made by different users. Excel provides a feature that highlights changes made to the workbook, allowing you to review them later.

1. Click **Review** > **Track Changes** > **Highlight Changes**.

2. Check **Track changes while editing** and configure options such as who made the changes and when.

3. Click **OK** to start tracking changes.

Managing Permissions

Excel allows you to control who can access and edit specific parts of a workbook. You can restrict access or set permission levels for different users.

1. Click **File** > **Info** > **Protect Workbook** > **Restrict Access**.

2. Set options like **Read-Only** or **Limit Editing**.

3. Assign specific users and define their permission levels.

Adding Comments and Notes

Adding comments or notes is a useful way to communicate with collaborators, ask questions, or leave reminders within a workbook.

1. Select a cell and click **Review** > **New Comment**.

2. Type your comment and click **Post**.

3. Other collaborators can reply to the comment.

Tip: Use **@mentions** in comments to notify specific users about important updates or queries.

Conclusion

Data validation and protection are critical tools in ensuring that your Excel spreadsheets maintain integrity, security, and accuracy. By applying data validation rules, you can prevent data entry errors and streamline workflows. Protecting worksheets and workbooks ensures that your data is safe from unauthorized modifications. Additionally, Excel's collaboration features allow teams to work together efficiently while maintaining control over access and changes.

Mastering these techniques will empower you to manage and share your data securely and effectively.

Chapter 11: Mastering Power Query for Data Transformation in Excel

Power Query in Excel is one of the most powerful tools for data manipulation. It helps users import, clean, reshape, and transform data with a high level of flexibility. Whether you're managing large datasets, automating repetitive tasks, or combining data from multiple sources, Power Query makes the process much more manageable.

In this chapter, we'll guide you through the essential aspects of Power Query, enabling you to transform and manage your data efficiently. We'll cover:

- How to import data from a variety of sources
- How to perform common transformations

- How to merge and append data from different queries for seamless integration

By the end of this chapter, you'll have the skills to streamline your data processing workflows and enhance your efficiency in Excel, allowing you to focus on analysis and decision-making rather than data preparation.

Importing Data from Multiple Sources

Power Query excels in its ability to connect to and import data from numerous sources, both local and online. You can easily integrate Excel files, CSVs, databases, web pages, and more. Let's look at how to get data into Power Query from various sources.

Key Sources for Data Import

1. **Excel Workbooks**: Import data from other workbooks, including sheets, named ranges, or tables.
2. **CSV and Text Files**: Import delimited text files like CSV, TXT, or TSV, which are often used for exporting data from other systems.

3. **Databases**: Whether you're working with SQL Server, Microsoft Access, or even Oracle, Power Query can connect to these databases and pull in tables or queries directly.

4. **Online Services**: SharePoint, Azure, and other cloud-based services can be linked to Power Query, enabling automatic updates from these online sources.

5. **Web Pages**: Extract data from web pages, such as tables or lists, that are publicly available.

6. **APIs and JSON/XML Files**: Power Query can fetch data from APIs and handle formats like JSON and XML for complex data sets.

Steps to Import Data Using Power Query

The process of importing data into Excel using Power Query is straightforward and user-friendly:

1. **Open Power Query Editor**:
   o In Excel, go to the **Data** tab and click **Get Data**.

- Choose from the list of available sources, such as **From File**, **From Database**, or **From Web**.

2. **Select the Source**:
   - After choosing your source, select the file, database, or API endpoint you wish to import.
   - A preview window will pop up where you can review your data.

3. **Preview and Load Data**:
   - The Power Query Navigator window lets you preview your data before loading it into Excel.
   - You can click **Load** to directly import it into a worksheet, or you can select **Transform Data** to open the data in Power Query Editor for further cleaning and transformation.

Pro Tip: If the data you're importing is from a source that updates frequently (like a sales database), you can set up Power Query to automatically refresh the data by clicking the **Refresh All** button in Excel, ensuring your workbook always contains the latest data.

Transforming Data with Power Query

Once your data is in Power Query, it's time to transform it. Power Query provides a rich set of features that help clean, format, and reshape your data, making it ready for analysis.

Common Data Transformations

1. **Removing Unnecessary Columns**:
   - Often, datasets contain columns that aren't relevant for analysis. Right-click on a column header, select **Remove Columns**, and eliminate any unnecessary data from your query.

2. **Filtering Rows**:
   - Power Query allows you to filter rows to only show data that meets certain criteria. Click the dropdown arrow in any column header to apply filters, such as

excluding rows with null values or filtering by specific dates or numbers.

3. **Splitting Columns**:

   o Data in a column might be combined in a way that isn't ideal for analysis. For example, if you have full names in one column, you might want to split them into first and last names. Power Query allows you to split columns based on delimiters, such as spaces, commas, or other custom criteria.

4. **Changing Data Types**:

   o Power Query automatically detects data types, but sometimes it may interpret data incorrectly (e.g., treating numbers as text). You can explicitly change a column's data type by selecting the column, clicking the **Transform** tab, and choosing the appropriate data type (such as **Text**, **Date**, **Number**, etc.).

5. **Filling Missing Data**:

- ○ Missing values can be replaced using the **Fill Down** or **Fill Up** options. This feature fills blank cells in a column by copying the data from adjacent rows, making sure your dataset is complete.

6. **Replacing Values**:
   - ○ Sometimes, you might want to replace specific values with new ones, such as fixing data errors or standardizing names. Power Query allows you to do this by selecting **Replace Values** from the **Transform** tab and entering the values to be replaced.

7. **Creating Calculated Columns**:
   - ○ You can create new columns based on existing data by using custom formulas. These formulas are written in Power Query's M language. To add a new calculated column, click the **Add Column** tab and choose **Custom Column**.

Managing Applied Steps

As you transform your data, Power Query records each change in the **Applied Steps** pane. This pane allows you to:

- **Rearrange** steps to modify the order in which transformations occur.
- **Edit** steps by clicking the gear icon next to each one.
- **Delete** any unwanted transformations by clicking the **X** next to the step.

Pro Tip: It's a good idea to minimize the number of steps to improve performance, as too many transformations can slow down your queries, especially with large datasets.

Merging and Appending Queries

When working with multiple datasets, combining them is often necessary. Power Query offers two primary methods to achieve this: merging and appending queries.

Merging Queries (Joins)

Merging is the process of combining two or more tables based on a common column, much like performing a JOIN operation in SQL. This is useful when you want to combine related data from different sources into one cohesive dataset.

Steps to Merge Queries

1. **Open Power Query Editor**:
   - In the **Data** tab, click **Get Data**, then choose **Combine Queries** and select **Merge Queries**.

2. **Select the Tables to Merge**:
   - Choose the primary table and the secondary table you want to merge.

3. **Identify the Key Column**:
   - Identify the column in each table that serves as the key for merging the data (e.g., Customer ID, Order Number).

4. **Choose the Join Type**:

- You can select from various join types: **Inner Join**, **Left Join**, **Right Join**, **Full Outer Join**, and others, depending on how you want the data to merge.

5. **Expand the Merged Table**:
   - After merging, you can expand the new column to display the data from the second table and select which columns you want to include.

Example: If you have a table of sales transactions and a table of customer information, you can merge them using a **Customer ID** to match the sales with the corresponding customer details.

Appending Queries (Stacking Data)

Appending is used to stack data from multiple tables that share the same column structure, such as combining monthly sales data into a single dataset.

Steps to Append Queries

1. **Open Power Query Editor**:

- Go to **Data > Get Data > Combine Queries**, then select **Append Queries**.

2. **Choose Tables to Append**:
   - Select the tables that you wish to combine. These tables should have identical column structures to ensure the data stacks correctly.

3. **Confirm and Load**:
   - Click **OK**, and the data will be appended into a single table, ready for analysis.

Example: If you receive monthly reports from different departments and want to consolidate them into one table, appending the data will save you time and effort.

Conclusion

Power Query is an indispensable tool for anyone looking to manage and transform data efficiently in Excel. With its robust features, it allows you to:

- Import data from various sources with ease.

- Clean and reshape data using a wide range of transformations.
- Merge and append data seamlessly from different queries.

By mastering Power Query, you'll drastically reduce the amount of time you spend on repetitive data preparation tasks, leaving you more time to focus on analysis and decision-making. Whether you're dealing with large datasets or automating workflows, Power Query is a game changer for any Excel user

Chapter 12: Power Pivot and Data Modeling in Excel

Power Pivot is an advanced feature in Microsoft Excel that enables users to handle large datasets, create sophisticated relationships between data tables, and perform powerful calculations using DAX (Data Analysis Expressions). For anyone working with complex data or large amounts of information, mastering Power Pivot can significantly improve your ability to analyze, summarize, and interpret data. In this chapter, we'll dive into the process of building data models, utilizing DAX functions, and creating advanced PivotTables to enhance your data analysis capabilities.

What is Power Pivot and Data Modeling?

Power Pivot is an Excel add-in that extends Excel's built-in data analysis functions. With Power Pivot, users can manage massive datasets, often exceeding

Excel's typical limitations, and create relationships between multiple tables, allowing for more efficient and accurate analysis. Unlike traditional PivotTables, which rely on a single dataset, Power Pivot allows you to pull data from multiple sources and build a model that can combine and analyze these datasets together.

Key Benefits of Power Pivot:

- **Handles large datasets**: Power Pivot is designed to work with large volumes of data, ensuring that performance doesn't degrade even with complex analysis.

- **Enables relational data models**: By creating relationships between tables, Power Pivot allows users to analyze related data from various sources within a single report.

- **Advanced calculations with DAX**: Power Pivot supports DAX, a specialized formula language, to create sophisticated custom calculations that go beyond what is possible with standard Excel formulas.

- **Enhanced reporting and analysis**: By building a data model, users can perform more complex analysis and generate insightful reports efficiently.

Power Pivot is particularly useful for business analysts, financial professionals, and anyone working with databases or large data sets that require in-depth analysis.

Creating Data Models in Power Pivot

A data model in Power Pivot is essentially a collection of related tables that can be combined in a PivotTable to analyze data more efficiently. Rather than relying on a single, large dataset, a data model allows you to break data into smaller, more manageable tables that are related through specific fields. This approach improves both performance and flexibility in handling data.

Steps to Create a Data Model:

1. **Loading Data into Power Pivot**
   - Start by opening Excel and navigating to the Power Pivot tab.
   - Click on **Manage** to open the Power Pivot window.
   - In this window, click **Get External Data** to import your datasets from various sources, such as Excel tables, databases, online data sources, or even CSV files.

2. **Creating Relationships Between Tables**
   - Once your data is imported, switch to **Diagram View** in Power Pivot.
   - In Diagram View, you can create relationships by dragging and dropping fields between different tables. For example, you might link a "Sales" table with a "Customers" table via a "CustomerID" field.
   - Ensure that relationships are established correctly, such as linking primary keys

(e.g., CustomerID) in one table with corresponding foreign keys in another (e.g., Sales.CustomerID).

3. **Adding Calculated Columns and Measures**

   o One of the most powerful features of Power Pivot is the ability to add calculated columns and measures using DAX formulas. Calculated columns are added to tables to generate new data based on existing columns, such as calculating the profit margin.

   o Measures, on the other hand, are dynamic calculations that summarize data. For example, a measure might calculate the total sales revenue or the average order value.

4. **Using the Data Model in PivotTables**

   o Once the data model is created, you can use it in Excel by inserting a PivotTable.

- In the **Insert PivotTable** dialog, select **Use an External Data Source** and choose the data model you just created.
- From there, drag and drop fields into rows, columns, values, and filters to perform your analysis.

Quick Tip: Instead of using traditional functions like VLOOKUP or INDEX-MATCH to pull data from different tables, Power Pivot's relationships allow you to connect multiple datasets seamlessly, improving performance and reliability.

Using DAX Functions

DAX (Data Analysis Expressions) is the language used in Power Pivot to create powerful custom calculations. Unlike regular Excel formulas, which operate on data in a worksheet, DAX formulas operate on data models. This allows for more dynamic and flexible calculations that automatically adjust based on the context of the PivotTable.

Common DAX Functions:

1. **Aggregations**
    - DAX allows you to perform standard aggregation functions such as SUM and AVERAGE. For example, SUM(Sales[Revenue]) adds up the revenue from a Sales table, while AVERAGE(Orders[Order Value]) calculates the average order value.

2. **Conditional Calculations**
    - DAX also supports conditional logic, enabling you to categorize or flag data based on specific conditions. For instance, you can use IF(Sales[Revenue] > 1000, "High", "Low") to categorize revenue into "High" or "Low" categories. Another example is SWITCH(Region[Code], 1, "North", 2, "South", "Other"), which assigns region names based on region codes.

3. **Time Intelligence**

- Power Pivot includes powerful time-based functions for analyzing data across different time periods. For example, TOTALYTD(SUM(Sales[Revenue]), Sales[Date]) calculates the total year-to-date revenue, while SAMEPERIODLASTYEAR(SUM(Sales[Revenue]), Sales[Date]) compares revenue for the same period in the previous year.

4. **Filtering and Context Manipulation**

- DAX also provides functions to manipulate the context of calculations and apply filters. CALCULATE(SUM(Sales[Revenue]), Sales[Region] = "West") calculates the sum of revenue but only for the "West" region. Similarly, FILTER(Orders, Orders[Order Date] > DATE(2023,1,1)) filters orders to include only those placed after January 1, 2023.

Quick Tip: DAX formulas are dynamic, meaning that when you change the context (such as adding a filter or slicing the data), the DAX formulas automatically recalculate, ensuring that your results are always up-to-date.

Building Advanced PivotTables with Power Pivot

Power Pivot's capabilities extend far beyond basic PivotTables, allowing users to create highly interactive and detailed PivotTables that can analyze complex datasets efficiently.

Steps to Build an Advanced PivotTable:

1. **Inserting a PivotTable Using the Data Model**
   - Navigate to the **Insert** tab and select **PivotTable**.
   - In the dialog box, choose **Use an External Data Source** and select your Power Pivot data model.
2. **Customizing the PivotTable Layout**

- After creating the PivotTable, you can drag fields into rows, columns, values, and filters.
- Customize your layout by sorting, grouping, and formatting the data as needed.
- For enhanced interactivity, add slicers and timelines to allow users to filter the data dynamically.

3. **Enhancing the PivotTable with DAX Measures**
   - Create custom measures in Power Pivot to calculate key performance indicators (KPIs), such as total sales, profit margins, or the average sales per customer. These dynamic measures will update automatically based on your PivotTable's context.

4. **Using PivotCharts for Data Visualization**

- PivotCharts provide a visual representation of your PivotTable data. After creating a PivotTable, you can insert a PivotChart to make your analysis more visually appealing and accessible.
- Using dynamic slicers with PivotCharts allows you to change the data displayed instantly, making it easier to analyze trends and outliers.

Quick Tip: Before loading data into Power Pivot, use Power Query to filter and clean your data. This reduces the load on Power Pivot and ensures better performance when analyzing large datasets.

Conclusion

Power Pivot is an essential tool for anyone working with large datasets or complex data analysis in Excel. By leveraging data models, creating relationships between tables, and using DAX functions for advanced calculations, you can transform Excel into a powerful business intelligence tool. Whether you're dealing with data from multiple sources, performing year-over-year comparisons, or creating interactive reports, Power Pivot provides the tools necessary to streamline your workflows and make data-driven decisions with confidence.

Mastering Power Pivot and Data Modeling in Excel unlocks a world of advanced analytical capabilities, helping you take your Excel skills to the next level and become a more efficient, data-savvy professional.

Week 4: Automation and Advanced Tools

Chapter 13: Introduction to Macros and VBA in Excel

Microsoft Excel is widely regarded as one of the most powerful tools available for organizing, analyzing, and presenting data. While Excel's built-in functions and formulas offer a vast array of possibilities for users, certain tasks, especially repetitive ones, can consume a significant amount of time. For tasks that require frequent repetition, Excel provides the solution in the form of Macros and VBA (Visual Basic for Applications). By leveraging these tools, users can significantly boost their productivity, automate time-consuming operations, and streamline complex workflows.

What Are Macros?

In its simplest form, a macro is a recorded sequence of actions that can be replayed to automate tasks. Instead of manually performing the same actions repeatedly, users can record a set of instructions once and then execute them with just a single click or keyboard shortcut. Macros save time and reduce the risk of human error, ensuring consistency across tasks, especially in scenarios where the same processes need to be applied repeatedly.

For example, imagine formatting reports by applying certain styles, adjusting column widths, changing font colors, and adjusting row heights. Rather than repeating this process every time, a macro can be recorded to perform all these formatting actions automatically. Similarly, macros can be used for other repetitive tasks such as importing data, generating reports, or applying specific calculations.

Recording and Running Macros in Excel

Excel makes it very easy to record macros without requiring any programming knowledge. You can record a macro and have it execute actions such as formatting, calculations, and data manipulation. Here's how to go about recording and running macros in Excel:

Step 1: Enabling the Developer Tab

Before you can start recording a macro, ensure the Developer tab is visible in Excel. By default, it's not enabled, so you must do the following to display it:

1. Open Excel and go to **File** > **Options**.
2. From the options window, select **Customize Ribbon**.
3. Under the **Main Tabs** section, check the box next to **Developer**.
4. Click **OK**. The Developer tab should now be visible on the ribbon at the top of your Excel window.

Step 2: Recording a Macro

Once the Developer tab is visible, you can start recording a macro by following these steps:

1. Click on the **Developer** tab.

2. In the **Code** section, click **Record Macro**.

3. Assign a name to your macro. Avoid using spaces; if necessary, use underscores or camelCase (e.g., "MyMacro").

4. Optionally, assign a shortcut key to quickly access the macro.

5. Choose where to store the macro:

   ○ **This Workbook**: The macro is available only within the current workbook.

   ○ **New Workbook**: The macro will be saved in a new Excel file.

   ○ **Personal Macro Workbook**: The macro can be accessed across all Excel files on your computer.

6. Click **OK** to start recording. From this point, Excel will track your actions and store them as part of the macro.

7. Perform the steps you want to automate. For example, you might format cells, copy data, or apply filters.

8. Once you've completed the desired actions, click **Stop Recording** in the Developer tab to save the macro.

Step 3: Running a Macro

To run a recorded macro:

1. Go to the **Developer** tab.
2. Click **Macros** in the Code section.
3. Select the macro you want to run from the list.
4. Click **Run** to execute the macro.

Alternatively, if you've assigned a keyboard shortcut to the macro, you can simply use that shortcut to execute it.

Editing and Customizing Macros

While recording macros is a great way to automate simple tasks, there will often be cases where you want to customize or refine the macro after recording. This is where VBA (Visual Basic for Applications) comes into play. Excel stores macros as

VBA code, which can be edited to achieve more complex or specific results.

Accessing the VBA Editor

To view and edit the VBA code behind your macro, follow these steps:

1. Click on the **Developer** tab.
2. Select **Visual Basic**, or simply press **ALT + F11** to open the VBA Editor.
3. In the VBA Editor, you will see a list of modules, which correspond to the macros you've recorded.

Modifying the Macro Code

Once you've accessed the VBA Editor, you can modify the macro's code to make adjustments. For instance, if you want to change the color of a cell, you could modify the VBA code like this:

```vba
Range("A1").Font.Color = RGB(255, 0, 0) 'This changes the font color to red
```

By changing the code, you can fine-tune how the macro behaves and add more complex functionalities that were not part of the original recording.

Writing Basic VBA Scripts

Recording macros is a quick way to automate basic tasks, but to unlock Excel's full automation potential, it's often necessary to write custom VBA scripts. With VBA, you can manipulate Excel objects, properties, and methods to achieve highly customized workflows. VBA uses a simple syntax that allows users to automate virtually any action within Excel.

Understanding VBA Syntax

The core of VBA consists of three main components:

- **Objects**: These are the elements you want to work with (e.g., a worksheet, a range of cells, a chart).
- **Properties**: These define the characteristics of the objects (e.g., font size, color, value).

- **Methods**: These are the actions you can perform on objects (e.g., copying, pasting, deleting).

Example of Writing a Simple VBA Script

Let's write a basic VBA script that enters text into a cell and formats it:

```vba
Sub FormatCell()
    ' Insert text into cell A1
    Range("A1").Value = "Hello, Excel!"

    ' Apply bold formatting to the text
    Range("A1").Font.Bold = True

    ' Change font size to 14
    Range("A1").Font.Size = 14

    ' Set the background color to yellow
    Range("A1").Interior.Color = RGB(255, 255, 0) 'Yellow
End Sub
```

This script demonstrates how to automate the process of entering data into a cell and applying formatting such as font size, color, and background color. By using VBA, you can add a high degree of customization to Excel tasks.

Common VBA Functions and Loops

In addition to simple scripts, VBA allows you to work with loops and conditional logic to automate more complex tasks. Let's look at some commonly used functions and control structures in VBA:

1. For Loop: Iterating Over a Range

```vba
Sub LoopThroughCells()
    Dim cell As Range
    For Each cell In Range("A1:A10")
        cell.Value = "Data " & cell.Row
    Next cell
End Sub
```

In this script, a **For Each** loop is used to iterate over each cell in the range A1:A10 and assign a value that includes the row number.

2. If Statements: Conditional Logic

```vba
Sub CheckValue()
    If Range("A1").Value > 100 Then
        MsgBox "Value exceeds 100!"
    Else
        MsgBox "Value is within limit."
    End If
End Sub
```

This script uses an **If** statement to check the value in cell A1. If the value exceeds 100, a message box appears, otherwise a different message box is shown.

Best Practices for Using Macros and VBA

To ensure that your macros and VBA scripts are reliable and efficient, it's important to follow a few best practices:

- **Always back up your data**: Before running any macro, make sure to save a backup of your workbook to avoid losing important data in case something goes wrong.

- **Use comments in your code**: Insert comments (') in your VBA scripts to explain what each part of the code does. This will make it easier to understand and modify the code later.

- **Test macros on sample data**: It's a good idea to test your macros and scripts on a smaller, non-critical workbook to ensure they work as expected.

- **Avoid excessive loops**: Be mindful of using loops, especially in large datasets. Unnecessarily large loops can significantly slow down performance in Excel.
- **Handle errors**: To avoid unexpected results, include error handling in your VBA scripts using the On Error statement:

```vba
On Error Resume Next
' Code that may cause an error
On Error GoTo 0
```

Conclusion

Macros and VBA are extremely powerful tools that can significantly improve your productivity in Excel. By automating repetitive tasks, macros save time and reduce the risk of human error. VBA takes this a step further by allowing you to write custom scripts for highly tailored solutions. Whether you are recording simple macros or writing complex VBA scripts, these tools can help you streamline workflows, handle large datasets, and perform advanced calculations with ease.

As you continue to experiment with macros and VBA, you will find that these tools not only save time but also help you uncover deeper insights and enhance your efficiency when working in Excel. Whether for personal projects or large-scale business processes, mastering macros and VBA will undoubtedly elevate your Excel skills and contribute to more effective data management.

Chapter 14: Using Excel with Python

Introduction

Microsoft Excel is a globally recognized tool for organizing, analyzing, and visualizing data. While Excel's built-in capabilities are powerful, the integration of Python allows users to extend its functionality, offering more advanced data analysis, automation, and machine learning possibilities.

Python's rich ecosystem of libraries makes it an ideal partner for enhancing Excel's features and enables users to perform complex tasks beyond the default Excel functions.

In this section, we will guide you through the process of setting up Python to work with Excel, using Python scripts to automate tasks, and analyzing data using Python's vast library support. By integrating Python with Excel, you can improve efficiency, increase productivity, and unlock new capabilities that will transform how you work with data.

Setting Up Python Integration with Excel

Before you can start using Python with Excel, you need to install the necessary tools and libraries. Below is a step-by-step guide to setting up the Python environment and preparing Excel to work with Python.

Step 1: Install Python

To use Python in Excel, you first need to have Python installed on your system. Python is not natively integrated into Excel, so installing it manually is a prerequisite. You can download and install the latest version of Python from the official Python website: python.org.

Step 2: Install Required Libraries

Python offers a variety of libraries that facilitate interaction with Excel files. The key libraries for working with Excel are:

1. **pandas**: A powerful library used for data manipulation and analysis. It allows you to load, modify, and export data from Excel files easily.

2. **openpyxl**: A library designed for working with Excel files in the .xlsx format, enabling you to read, write, and modify the data in these files.

3. **xlrd**: A library for reading older Excel files in the .xls format.

4. **xlwt**: A library for writing data to .xls files (older Excel format).

5. **XlsxWriter**: A library used for creating and writing to .xlsx files with advanced formatting capabilities.

To install these libraries, you can use Python's package manager, **pip**. Run the following command in your terminal or command prompt:

```bash
pip install pandas openpyxl xlrd xlwt XlsxWriter
```

Step 3: Set Up Jupyter Notebook (Optional)

For an interactive experience, many users opt to use **Jupyter Notebook** to write and execute Python code. Jupyter Notebook allows you to write Python scripts in a cell-based interface, which makes it easier to test and visualize code.

You can install Jupyter Notebook with pip:

```bash
pip install notebook
```

To start Jupyter Notebook, run the following command in the terminal:

```bash
jupyter notebook
```

This will launch a web interface where you can create, edit, and run Python scripts interactively.

Writing Python Scripts within Excel

Excel offers several ways to integrate Python for scripting purposes. One of the most popular methods is through the **PyXLL** add-in, which allows you to write Python code directly within Excel. Below is a guide on how to set up PyXLL and use it to run Python code within Excel.

Using Python in Excel with PyXLL

PyXLL is an Excel add-in that allows users to execute Python code from within Excel, providing an easy way to integrate Python functions and capabilities. It allows for seamless communication between Python scripts and Excel worksheets.

To install PyXLL, use the following pip command:

```bash
pip install pyxll
```

To activate the PyXLL add-in in Excel, follow these steps:

1. Open Excel and go to **File > Options**.
2. In the Excel options, click on **Add-ins**.
3. Select **Manage COM Add-ins** and click on **Go**.
4. In the pop-up window, check the box next to **PyXLL** to enable the add-in.

Once PyXLL is enabled, you can start writing Python code directly within Excel.

Running Python Scripts in Excel

With Python integrated into Excel, you can start running scripts that interact with Excel data. The **pandas** library is often used to read, manipulate, and write Excel files in Python.

Reading an Excel File with pandas

The first step in any Excel-related task is typically reading data from an existing Excel file. The following Python code demonstrates how to read data from an Excel file using pandas:

```python
import pandas as pd

# Load the Excel file
excel_data = pd.read_excel("data.xlsx")

# Display the first few rows of the dataset
print(excel_data.head())
```

This script will load an Excel file named data.xlsx and print the first five rows of data.

Writing Data to an Excel File with pandas

You can also write data back to an Excel file. For instance, the following code creates a new DataFrame with some data and saves it to an Excel file:

```python
import pandas as pd

# Create a DataFrame
data = {"Name": ["Alice", "Bob"], "Score": [85, 90]}
df = pd.DataFrame(data)

# Write the DataFrame to an Excel file
df.to_excel("output.xlsx", index=False)
```

This will create a new file called output.xlsx with the data.

Automating Excel with Python

With Python's libraries such as **openpyxl**, you can automate more complex tasks in Excel, such as modifying cell values or applying formatting. These tasks can save you time and effort when working with large datasets.

Changing Cell Values Programmatically

Here is an example that demonstrates how to change a cell's value using openpyxl:

```python
from openpyxl import load_workbook

# Load the Excel workbook
wb = load_workbook("data.xlsx")

# Select the active sheet
sheet = wb.active

# Change the value of cell A1
sheet["A1"] = "Updated Value"

# Save the workbook with the updated value
wb.save("data.xlsx")
```

Formatting Cells in Excel

Python can also automate formatting tasks in Excel. For example, the following code formats cell A1 to display bold text in red:

```python
from openpyxl.styles import Font

# Change the font style of cell A1
sheet["A1"].font = Font(bold=True, color="FF0000")

# Save the changes
wb.save("data.xlsx")
```

188

Analyzing Data Using Python Libraries

Python's libraries provide powerful tools for advanced data analysis and visualization. You can use **pandas**, **NumPy**, and **Matplotlib** for data analysis, statistical calculations, and creating visualizations.

Using pandas for Data Analysis

Pandas is a go-to library for data manipulation. The following code shows how to use pandas to describe a dataset:

```python
import pandas as pd

# Load data from Excel
df = pd.read_excel("data.xlsx")

# Get a summary of the dataset
print(df.describe())
```

This will output descriptive statistics of the data, including mean, median, standard deviation, and more.

Visualizing Data with Matplotlib

Matplotlib is a popular library for creating visualizations. For example, to create a bar chart based on the data:

```python
import matplotlib.pyplot as plt

# Plot a bar chart
df.plot(kind='bar', x='Name', y='Score')

# Display the plot
plt.show()
```

This code will generate a bar chart that displays the scores for each name in the dataset.

Performing Calculations with NumPy

NumPy is ideal for performing mathematical operations on data. Below is an example of calculating the mean score from the dataset:

```python
import numpy as np

# Convert the scores column to a NumPy array
scores = np.array(df["Score"])

# Calculate and print the mean score
print("Mean Score:", np.mean(scores))
```

Conclusion

By integrating Python with Excel, you can significantly enhance your data analysis, automation, and reporting capabilities. Python's rich set of libraries such as pandas, openpyxl, NumPy, and Matplotlib provide an efficient and powerful way to manipulate, analyze, and visualize data. Whether you are automating tasks, performing complex data analysis, or generating reports, Python adds a new dimension to Excel, allowing you to streamline your workflow and perform tasks more efficiently.

By leveraging Python and Excel together, you will be equipped to handle a variety of data-centric tasks, from basic operations to sophisticated data science and machine learning workflows. Start experimenting with these tools, and see how Python can revolutionize the way you work with Excel.

Chapter 15: Leveraging AI with Copilot in Excel

Introduction

Microsoft Excel has long been one of the most powerful tools for organizing, analyzing, and visualizing data. Traditionally, users have relied on its extensive array of formulas, functions, and features to manipulate data. However, the introduction of AI-powered features like **Copilot** has taken Excel to a whole new level. With Copilot integrated into Microsoft 365, users can now tap into the power of artificial intelligence to automate repetitive tasks, generate deeper insights from data, and improve overall productivity.

Copilot utilizes advanced machine learning models and natural language processing to assist with tasks that once required technical expertise, making complex data tasks simpler and more efficient.

This section will explore the core features of Copilot in Excel, explain how it can automate various tasks, and showcase how AI-powered assistance can revolutionize data analysis and reporting. Whether you're a beginner or an advanced Excel user, you'll find that Copilot is designed to optimize your workflow, saving time and enhancing your decision-making process.

Overview of Copilot Features

Microsoft Copilot for Excel is built into the Microsoft 365 ecosystem, providing users with AI-driven capabilities that streamline everyday tasks. Through machine learning and natural language processing, Copilot enables users to interact with data in ways that were once complicated and time-consuming. Below are some key features of Copilot in Excel that can significantly improve your workflow.

1. **Natural Language Data Interaction**

One of the most revolutionary aspects of Copilot is its ability to interact with Excel using natural language commands. Users no longer have to memorize complex formulas or manually search for the right function. Instead, they can simply type commands in plain language, and Copilot will translate these requests into the appropriate Excel actions. For example:

"Show me the top 5 regions with the highest sales in Q1."

Copilot will process the data, identify the correct criteria, and display the results in seconds, all without requiring the user to write complicated formulas or manipulate the data manually.

2. **Automated Formula Generation**

Excel is known for its powerful array of formulas and functions, but for some users, manually creating these formulas can be a daunting task. Copilot simplifies this process by automatically generating the required formulas based on user input. For example, if you ask:

"Calculate the total revenue per product category,"

Copilot will create and insert the appropriate formula, such as **SUMIF** or **PivotTable** functions, based on the dataset and the user's request. This eliminates the need for users to manually enter or troubleshoot formulas.

3. **Data Insights and Trend Analysis**

Copilot is also capable of performing sophisticated data analysis, uncovering insights, identifying trends, and spotting anomalies that would be time-consuming to find manually. By processing large datasets and applying machine learning techniques, Copilot can offer valuable insights. For instance, you might ask:

"What are the key trends in this sales data?"

Copilot will analyze the dataset, detect correlations, and visualize trends in charts, presenting users with a clear understanding of the data's underlying patterns.

4. Automatic Chart Creation

While creating charts and graphs manually in Excel can be a time-consuming process, Copilot streamlines this by automatically generating visualizations based on your data and commands. For example, you could type:

"Create a line graph showing monthly sales figures."

Copilot will automatically select the relevant data, format it into a line graph, and present it to you, saving you time and effort in the process of data visualization.

5. Smart Data Cleaning

One of the most challenging aspects of working with data is dealing with messy or inconsistent data. Copilot assists with data cleaning by automatically identifying duplicates, standardizing formats, and suggesting fixes for errors. For instance, if your data contains inconsistent date formats, you can command:

"Fix the date format in this dataset."

Copilot will standardize the date formats across your entire worksheet, ensuring that all data is consistent and correctly formatted. It can also automatically detect and remove duplicate entries, making the process of cleaning data much faster and more accurate.

Automating Tasks with Copilot Actions

Repetitive tasks such as data entry, formatting, and report generation are common in Excel, often consuming valuable time. Copilot can automate these tasks, allowing you to focus on more strategic activities while improving efficiency. Here are several ways Copilot can help automate these processes:

1. **Automating Data Entry and Formatting**

Copilot can reduce the effort required for manual data entry and formatting. By recognizing patterns in your data, it can autofill missing values and format data columns as required. You can also automate the application of styles such as currency, percentages, or dates. For example, you could command:

"Format this table with alternating row colors and bold headers."

Copilot will immediately apply the specified formatting, making your table more readable and visually appealing. This saves hours of manual formatting.

2. Instant Report Generation

Creating reports manually is often a multi-step process that involves gathering data, summarizing key metrics, and formatting. With Copilot, all of these tasks can be streamlined. For instance, you might say:

"Generate a monthly sales performance report."

Copilot will gather the necessary data, analyze the metrics, and produce a fully formatted report with tables, charts, and actionable insights. This significantly speeds up the process of creating high-quality reports.

3. **Automating Data Validation and Error Checking**

Data errors can undermine the quality of your analysis, but with Copilot, identifying and correcting mistakes becomes much easier. Copilot can automatically check for missing or incorrect values and suggest corrections. For example, you could ask:

"Highlight all entries where sales revenue is below $500."

Copilot will apply conditional formatting to highlight those rows, helping you quickly identify discrepancies. It can also check for other types of data issues, such as inconsistent units of measurement or incorrect date formats.

4. **Scheduling Tasks and Workflows**

Copilot integrates with Microsoft Power Automate, enabling users to schedule Excel-related tasks and workflows. For instance, you could automate the process of sending reports via email, updating databases with new data, or setting reminders for important tasks. This integration reduces the need for manual intervention and ensures that your workflows are consistent and timely.

Enhancing Data Analysis with AI Assistance

Copilot's capabilities extend far beyond basic data entry and formatting. It also offers advanced data analysis features that can help users perform sophisticated tasks without the need for in-depth statistical knowledge. Here's a closer look at how Copilot can elevate your data analysis experience:

1. **Predictive Analytics**

One of the standout features of Copilot is its ability to perform predictive analytics. By leveraging historical data, Copilot can forecast future trends and make predictions. For example, you could request:

"Predict next quarter's sales based on historical data."

Copilot will analyze the data, apply predictive models, and provide a forecast for the next quarter, allowing businesses to make data-driven decisions with greater confidence.

2. Sentiment Analysis on Customer Feedback

Analyzing customer feedback is crucial for understanding customer sentiment. Copilot can automatically perform sentiment analysis on large datasets of customer reviews, categorizing feedback as positive, neutral, or negative. You might ask:

"Analyze customer feedback and summarize sentiment trends."

Copilot will process the feedback, identify patterns, and offer a summary of the sentiment trends, helping businesses understand their customers' perceptions.

3. **Correlation and Pattern Detection**

Identifying relationships between different variables is a common challenge in data analysis. Copilot can detect correlations between various datasets without requiring users to run complex statistical tests. For example:

"Find the correlation between marketing spend and sales."

Copilot will calculate the correlation and present it in an easy-to-understand format, allowing you to quickly identify relationships and trends.

4. **PivotTables with AI Assistance**

PivotTables are a powerful feature in Excel for summarizing large datasets. However, they can be difficult to set up correctly. With Copilot, you can easily generate PivotTables by typing commands like:

"Create a PivotTable summarizing sales by region and product category."

Copilot will instantly generate the PivotTable and format it according to your request, enabling users to extract valuable insights from large datasets.

5. Anomaly Detection

In large datasets, anomalies and outliers can be hard to spot manually. Copilot uses advanced AI techniques to identify data points that deviate significantly from the norm. You might ask:

"Identify any unusual sales figures in this dataset."

Copilot will flag any anomalies, allowing you to quickly investigate potential issues or opportunities in the data.

Conclusion

Microsoft Copilot for Excel is a groundbreaking tool that takes data analysis and productivity to a whole new level. By leveraging artificial intelligence, Copilot automates repetitive tasks, generates deep insights from data, and simplifies complex processes such as predictive analytics and anomaly detection. Whether you're creating reports, cleaning data, or performing advanced statistical analysis, Copilot acts as an intelligent assistant that helps you make smarter, data-driven decisions.

With Copilot integrated into Excel, professionals can save time, reduce errors, and unlock valuable insights that were once difficult to uncover. As AI technology continues to advance, tools like Copilot will become even more essential for businesses and individuals who want to stay ahead of the curve in data analysis and decision-making.

If you haven't explored Copilot in Excel yet, now is the perfect time to embrace this powerful tool. By leveraging AI to assist with everyday tasks, you'll be able to boost your productivity and take your Excel skills to the next level!

Chapter 16: Optimizing Performance and Troubleshooting in Excel

Introduction

Microsoft Excel is one of the most widely used software applications for data analysis, organization, and calculation. However, as workbooks grow in complexity, Excel users can encounter performance challenges. Slow load times, unresponsive formulas, or even application crashes can become frustrating, especially when managing large datasets. Additionally, common Excel issues, such as formula errors or corrupted files, can impede work and lower productivity.

In this section, we will provide you with a comprehensive guide to optimizing the performance of your Excel workbooks. We will also cover strategies for troubleshooting common issues to ensure that your Excel experience remains smooth and efficient. By following the tips and techniques outlined here, you can enhance both the speed and reliability of your Excel workbooks, enabling you to manage even the most complex datasets with ease.

Improving Workbook Efficiency

As the size and complexity of your Excel workbooks increase, it's essential to optimize their efficiency to ensure smooth performance. Below are some key strategies for improving workbook performance:

1. Reduce File Size

One of the primary causes of sluggish Excel performance is excessive file size. Large files can slow down Excel's responsiveness and increase the risk of crashes. Here are several ways to reduce your workbook's file size:

- **Remove Unnecessary Formatting**: Conditional formatting, excessive colors, and unused styles can increase the file size. By cleaning up these elements, you can make your workbook leaner.

- **Compress Images**: If your workbook contains images, consider using Excel's built-in compression tools to reduce their file size without compromising quality.

- **Delete Unused Worksheets**: Extra sheets that do not contain useful data can unnecessarily inflate the size of your workbook. Be sure to remove any unused sheets.

- **Save as Excel Binary File (.xlsb)**: Excel's binary format (.xlsb) is optimized for large data sets. If your workbook contains a substantial amount of data, saving it as a .xlsb file can help improve performance.

2. Optimize Formulas

Excel formulas are essential for data analysis, but complex formulas can slow down calculations. To improve performance, consider the following:

- **Replace Volatile Functions**: Volatile functions like NOW(), TODAY(), RAND(), and OFFSET() recalculate every time the workbook is updated, which can slow down performance. If frequent updates are not required, replace these functions with static values.

- **Use Helper Columns**: Instead of writing lengthy nested formulas, break them down into simpler steps using helper columns. This can make calculations faster and easier to manage.

- **Minimize Array Formulas**: While array formulas are powerful, they can be computationally expensive, especially with large datasets. Whenever possible, replace array formulas with simpler alternatives, such as PivotTables or regular formulas.

- **Use Structured References**: Excel Tables are optimized for performance, so convert your data ranges into tables (Ctrl + T). This improves performance and ensures automatic updating when new data is added.

3. Turn Off Automatic Calculation (When Necessary)

In workbooks with numerous formulas, automatic recalculation can significantly slow down Excel's performance. Switching to manual calculation mode helps mitigate this issue.

- **To turn off automatic calculation**:
    1. Go to the **Formulas** tab.
    2. Under **Calculation Options**, select **Manual**.
    3. Press F9 to manually recalculate your workbook when needed.

4. Use Named Ranges and Tables

By defining **Named Ranges** or converting data into **Excel Tables**, you can simplify your formulas and improve performance. This approach makes your formulas more efficient and easier to manage, particularly when dealing with large datasets.

5. Minimize External Links

External links to other workbooks or files can slow down Excel's performance, especially when the linked files are located on remote servers or network drives. Consolidating your data into one workbook can reduce these external dependencies and improve performance.

Troubleshooting Common Excel Issues

As powerful as Excel is, users may encounter issues that disrupt their workflow. Below are some common problems and their solutions:

1. Excel Running Slow or Freezing

Several factors can cause Excel to run slowly or freeze:

- **Too Many Formulas**: A high volume of formulas can drain resources. Replace formulas with static values where possible to improve performance.

- **Excessive Conditional Formatting**: Conditional formatting can slow down workbook performance, especially when applied across large ranges. Simplify or remove unnecessary rules.

- **Large Data Ranges**: If you're working with a large dataset, consider splitting the data across multiple sheets or reducing the range of data being analyzed.

- **Corrupt Workbook**: Sometimes, a workbook might become corrupted, leading to performance issues. To check if the issue is related to corruption, try opening Excel in Safe Mode (Ctrl + Excel Icon > Open in Safe Mode) and see if the problem persists.

2. Excel Crashes or Doesn't Respond

If Excel crashes or becomes unresponsive, try the following fixes:

- **Update Excel**: Ensure you are using the latest version of Excel. Microsoft frequently releases updates that fix bugs and improve stability.

- **Disable Add-ins**: Some add-ins may cause Excel to crash. Go to **File > Options > Add-ins** and disable any unnecessary add-ins.

- **Check for File Corruption**: If a specific file causes Excel to crash, try repairing it. Open Excel, go to **File > Open**, select the file, click the dropdown arrow beside "Open," and choose **Open and Repair**.

- **Increase Virtual Memory**: If your virtual memory is set too low, it may lead to crashes. To adjust this, go to **System Properties > Advanced > Performance Settings** on Windows.

3. Formula Errors

Formula errors can be caused by various issues. Here's how to troubleshoot common formula errors:

- **VALUE!**: This error often occurs when incorrect data types are used in formulas. Check for mismatched data types.

- **REF!**: This error indicates that a referenced cell has been deleted or is no longer valid.

- **DIV/0!**: This error occurs when a formula attempts division by zero. To avoid this, use IFERROR(A1/B1, "Error") to handle errors gracefully.

- **NAME?**: This error usually means that a function name is misspelled or a named range is missing. Double-check for any typos.

4. Excel File Won't Open

If an Excel file won't open, consider the following troubleshooting steps:

- **Open in Safe Mode**: Try opening the file in Safe Mode by holding Ctrl while opening the Excel icon.

- **Check File Permissions**: Ensure that you have the necessary permissions to open the file, particularly if it's stored on a network drive.

- **Unblock the File**: Sometimes, files downloaded from the internet are blocked. Right-click the file, select **Properties**, and check the box that says **Unblock**.

- **Try an Older Version**: If a recent Excel update causes issues, try opening the file in an older version of Excel.

5. PivotTables Not Refreshing Correctly

PivotTables may not refresh automatically, leading to outdated data. Here's how to resolve this issue:

- **Ensure Data Source is Correct**: Check that the data source for the PivotTable is valid and up to date.

- **Refresh Manually**: If the PivotTable does not refresh automatically, press Alt + F5 to refresh it manually.

- **Check for Filters**: Filters can sometimes interfere with PivotTable refresh. Ensure that filters aren't affecting the data displayed in your PivotTable.

Best Practices for Working with Large Datasets

Handling large datasets in Excel can be tricky, but by following these best practices, you can ensure optimal performance and accuracy:

1. Use Efficient Data Structures

Converting raw data into Excel Tables (Ctrl + T) is a powerful way to improve efficiency. Excel Tables automatically format and filter your data, making it easier to manage and analyze.

2. Reduce Formula Complexity

Avoid using large, complex formulas. Instead, try to use more efficient functions like LOOKUP, VLOOKUP, or XLOOKUP. These functions are faster and easier to manage than large IF statements.

3. Enable Data Filtering and Sorting

Excel's AutoFilter tool (Ctrl + Shift + L) is invaluable when working with large datasets. It allows you to quickly find the data you need without scrolling through endless rows.

4. Use Power Query for Data Processing

Power Query is a robust tool for importing, cleaning, and transforming data. It allows you to perform complex data manipulation without slowing down your workbook. Power Query can significantly speed up data processing tasks and is ideal for preparing data for analysis.

5. Use Power Pivot for Large Data Models

When dealing with massive datasets, Power Pivot can help manage relationships and perform complex calculations without causing Excel to slow down. To enable Power Pivot, go to **File > Options > Add-ins** and enable the Power Pivot COM Add-in.

6. Optimize Charts and Dashboards

Avoid using too many real-time updating charts, as they can slow down workbook performance. Instead, use **PivotCharts** for more efficient visualizations of large datasets. Limit the use of animated elements in charts, as these can reduce the overall speed.

7. Split Data Across Multiple Sheets or Files

If your dataset exceeds Excel's row limit (1,048,576 rows per sheet), consider splitting the data across multiple sheets. Alternatively, for very large datasets, consider using a database system such as **Microsoft Access** or **SQL Server** for data storage.

Conclusion

By following these tips and techniques, you can optimize your Excel workbooks for better performance and reliability. Whether you're dealing with complex formulas, large datasets, or common errors, implementing these strategies will help you avoid frustration and work more efficiently. Optimize your workbooks today and take your Excel skills to the next level, ensuring a faster, more responsive, and error-free experience.

Appendices and Glossary

Appendices

Appendix A: Keyboard Shortcuts

Utilizing keyboard shortcuts can greatly improve your productivity in Excel. Below is a categorized collection of essential shortcuts that will help you navigate and manipulate your workbooks more efficiently:

General Shortcuts

- **Ctrl + N** – Create a new workbook
- **Ctrl + O** – Open an existing workbook
- **Ctrl + S** – Save the workbook
- **F12** – Open the Save As dialog box
- **Ctrl + P** – Print the current worksheet
- **Ctrl + Z** – Undo the last action
- **Ctrl + Y** – Redo the last undone action

Navigation and Selection

- **Arrow Keys** – Move one cell in the direction of the arrow

- **Ctrl + Arrow Key** – Jump to the edge of the data range
- **Ctrl + Home** – Move to the top-left corner of the worksheet
- **Ctrl + End** – Jump to the last used cell
- **Shift + Space** – Select the entire row
- **Ctrl + Space** – Select the entire column
- **Ctrl + A** – Select all cells in the worksheet

Editing and Formatting

- **Ctrl + C** – Copy selected cells
- **Ctrl + X** – Cut selected cells
- **Ctrl + V** – Paste copied or cut data
- **Ctrl + B** – Apply bold formatting
- **Ctrl + I** – Apply italic formatting
- **Ctrl + U** – Apply underline formatting
- **Ctrl + 1** – Open the Format Cells dialog box
- **Alt + Enter** – Insert a line break within a cell

Formulas and Functions

- **F2** – Edit the active cell's content

- **Alt + =** – AutoSum (quickly adds up selected numbers)
- **F4** – Repeat the last action or toggle between absolute and relative references in formulas
- **Ctrl + `** – Show or hide formulas in the worksheet
- **Shift + F3** – Open the Insert Function dialog box

Working with Data

- **Ctrl + T** – Convert a range of data into a table
- **Ctrl + Shift + L** – Apply or remove filters from data
- **Alt + D + F + F** – Open the Advanced Filter options
- **F9** – Recalculate all formulas in the workbook

Appendix B: Excel Resources and Communities

Official Microsoft Resources

- <u>Microsoft Excel Support</u> – Official resources and tutorials from Microsoft
- <u>Excel Help & Learning</u> – Online tutorials and courses offered by Microsoft
- <u>Microsoft Excel Community</u> – A place to connect with other Excel users and experts

Online Learning Platforms

- **LinkedIn Learning** – Offers Excel courses ranging from beginner to advanced
- **Coursera** – Provides courses from top universities focused on Excel
- **Udemy** – Offers a wide range of Excel tutorials, from basic to advanced topics

Popular Excel Forums and Communities

- **Reddit Excel Community (<u>r/excel</u>)** – A thriving forum for Excel questions and solutions
- **MrExcel Forum (<u>www.mrexcel.com</u>)** – A forum for solving complex Excel problems, including VBA and formulas

- **Stack Overflow (stackoverflow.com)** – A comprehensive Q&A site for advanced Excel techniques, including VBA

Appendix C: Sample Data Sets for Practice

Practicing with real-world sample data is an effective way to enhance your Excel skills. Below are some resources to obtain sample datasets:

Preloaded Excel Templates

Excel provides numerous built-in templates with sample data. To access them:

1. Open Excel and go to **File > New**
2. Search for templates such as "Budget," "Sales Report," or "Employee Attendance"
3. Download and modify the template for your practice

Publicly Available Datasets

- Kaggle – A wide selection of datasets for data analysis and visualization

- [Google Dataset Search](#) – A tool for finding datasets from various sources
- [FiveThirtyEight](#) – Provides real-world datasets from journalism and research

Manually Created Sample Data

Here is an example of a simple dataset you can practice with:

Employee ID	Name	Department	Salary	Hire Date
1001	Alice	Finance	$60,000	2018-06-10
1002	Bob	IT	$75,000	2019-03-22
1003	Carol	Marketing	$50,000	2020-09-15
1004	David	HR	$55,000	2021-12-01
1005	Emma	Sales	$65,000	2017-07-30

This dataset can be used to practice a variety of Excel functions, including SUM(), AVERAGE(), IF(), and VLOOKUP(), as well as PivotTables and charts.

Glossary

A

- **Absolute Reference** – A reference that remains constant when copied to other cells (e.g., A1).
- **Array Formula** – A formula that processes multiple calculations at once and returns an array of values.
- **AutoFill** – A feature that automatically fills in values based on a recognized pattern.

B

- **Binary Workbook (.xlsb)** – A file format that saves Excel workbooks in binary form, improving performance.
- **Break Links** – A function used to remove external links from a workbook.

C

- **Cell** – The intersection point of a row and a column in a worksheet.
- **Conditional Formatting** – A tool for applying formatting based on the values in a cell.

D

- **Data Validation** – A feature that restricts the type of data entered into a cell.
- **Dynamic Arrays** – A feature that allows a formula to return multiple results in a "spill" range.

F

- **Formula Bar** – The area at the top of Excel that displays the content of the selected cell.
- **Freeze Panes** – A feature that allows you to lock rows or columns for easier scrolling.

M

- **Macro** – A recorded set of actions used to automate repetitive tasks.
- **Merge Cells** – A feature that combines multiple cells into one.

P

- **PivotTable** – A tool used for summarizing and analyzing large datasets dynamically.
- **Power Query** – A tool for importing, transforming, and cleaning data.

R

- **Relative Reference** – A reference that adjusts when copied to other cells.
- **Range** – A selection of multiple cells in a worksheet.

V

- **VBA (Visual Basic for Applications)** – A programming language used to automate tasks in Excel.
- **VLOOKUP** – A function that searches for a value in one column and returns related data from another column.

This glossary serves as a quick reference for essential Excel terminology. Mastering these concepts will help you work more efficiently and effectively in Excel as you continue to advance your skills.

www.ingramcontent.com/pod-product-compliance
Lightning Source LLC
La Vergne TN
LVHW022340060326
832902LV00022B/4159